Hypothesis 891

Beyond the Roadblocks

Colectivo Situaciones & MTD Solano

Minor Compositions

Translated by Dina Khorasanee & Liz Mason-Deese

Hypothesis 891. Beyond the Roadblocks
Colectivo Situaciones & MTD Solano
Translated by Dina Khorasanee & Liz Mason-Deese
ISBN 978-1-57027-217-2

Cover design by Haduhi Szukis
Interior design by Casandra Johns (www.houseofhands.net)

Copyedited by Joanna Figiel

Released by Minor Compositions 2023
Colchester / New York / Port Watson

Minor Compositions is a series of interventions & provocations drawing from
autonomous politics, avant-garde aesthetics, and the revolutions of everyday life.

Minor Compositions is an imprint of Autonomedia
www.minorcompositions.info
minorcompositions@gmail.com

Distributed by Autonomedia
PO Box 568 Williamsburgh Station
Brooklyn, NY 11211

www.autonomedia.org
info@autonomedia.org

Contents

Translator's Introduction

Hypothesis 891 is precisely that – a series of situated hypotheses (the number comes from the street address where those hypotheses were elaborated). It also showcases the *process* through which those hypotheses were proposed, discussed, tested, challenged, accepted or discarded. In other words, it does not present *answers*, but a way of asking questions. In this sense it represents a process of "militant research" or "research militancy." These texts were part of a series of workshops held with members of the militant research collective Colectivo Situaciones and members of the *Movimiento de Trabajadores Desocupados* [Unemployed Workers' Movement, MTD] of Solano. At the time, Colectivo Situaciones consisted of a group of university students who had become frustrated with the dominant forms of leftist activism and academic knowledge. In search of a form of knowledge immanent to struggles, and one that did not separate the object from the subject of knowledge production, they began working with the series of innovative social movements emerging in Argentina to collectively reflect on and theorize the moment, recognizing, in turn, that this knowledge is itself a productive force that intervenes in the situation at hand. The work presented here brings Colectivo Situaciones into dialogue with one of the most innovative movements of the unemployed at the time: the MTD of Solano. The MTD of Solano was already developing its own conceptions of autonomy, power, neighborhood organizing, alternative economies, the production of subjectivity, the meaning of freedom. The confluence between the two groups thus produced immensely rich dialogue, which extended well beyond the production of this book.

The texts that make up this book include initial hypotheses, written by Colectivo Situaciones, edited transcripts of the conversations in the workshops discussing the hypotheses, and response pieces by both Colectivo Situaciones and the MTD of Solano. The book as a whole is the result of a process of collective thought and elaboration, by each group on its own – Colectivo Situaciones and the MTD of Solano – and together through workshop discussions where the words of members of each collective are woven together to create new understandings and analyses that could not have emerged from either collective alone. The texts thus reflect tensions, both between and within the collectives, and also elaborations on those tensions as the thinking changes over time.

The workshops that provided the material for this book took place between September 2001 and August 2002, during which time Argentina saw one of the most important processes of resistance to neoliberal capitalism that the world had seen at that time, effectively overthrowing the neoliberal government in December 2001. That uprising was led by many of the movements and organizations discussed in this book – the movements of the unemployed, neighborhood assemblies, and barter networks – but it also exceeded and went far beyond those existing forms of organizing. It drew all sorts of people into the streets, despite the state of emergency and curfew declared by the government. Those people, whether in organizations or not, protested, set up barricades and fought off the police and military, until the president, Fernando de la Rúa, abandoned his office. This was followed by a period of intense social experimentation, both in forms of political organization and in forms of researching and thinking, of which this book is a prime example.

"A movement of movements": The Unemployed Workers' Organizations

By the late 1990s, Argentina was experiencing a severe economic crisis: years of neoliberal structural adjustment, demanded by the International Monetary Fund and the World Bank, had failed and poverty and unemployment were reaching record levels. It was in this context that the unemployed began organizing. At first derided and ignored by the major labor union federations and leftist parties alike, the unemployed began organizing autonomously, initially coming together around shared problems of social reproduction – unpayable electricity and gas bills, the rising cost of food, health care, and education – and mass job loss. In smaller cities in the interior of the country, such as Cultral-Có, whole communities came together after mass layoffs at the recently privatized oil company YPF. These uprisings – known as *pueblazos* for the way the whole community participated – were fundamental in bringing the issue of unemployment into the public agenda and popularizing the tactic of the roadblock (*piquete*). As the unemployed began organizing around the country, from those smaller cities to the urban peripheries of major metropolises such as Buenos Aires, La Plata, and Rosario, the tactic of the roadblock became the tool of choice for the unemployed. This is what led to the organized unemployed being known as *piqueteros*.[1] Organizations of the unemployed – *piqueterxs* – thus started organizing roadblocks around the country, blockading major highways, bridges, and other key transit points, sometimes for weeks at a time. Those roadblocks brought the circulation of commodities to a halt and forced different levels of government to start responding to the *piqueterxs* demands for unemployment insurance, food aid, etc. The roadblocks, at least in some cases, were also a space for what the MTD of Solano refers to as the construction of a "new sociality," producing new ways of living together that challenge the dominant capitalist subjectivity.

Despite this shared tactic and common problems, the different organizations of the unemployed that emerged in different territories were extremely diverse, with different compositions, adopting different ideological positions and organizational forms, and making different alliances. As the political power of the unemployed became clear, labor unions and leftist parties also started their own unemployed branches or tried to bring existing unemployed organizations into their fold. And yet, other unemployed organizations remained "autonomous," unaffiliated with any major unions, parties, or other social organizations. Those autonomous organizations generally took the name of *Movimiento de Trabajadores Desocupados* [Unemployed Workers' Movement] of their given territory. The MTD of Solano, a locality in the southern part of Buenos Aires' urban periphery, was one of these. The organization initially emerged from meetings at a local parish and then, after being evicted from the parish by the bishop, expanded to bring together different neighborhood groups of the unemployed across the territory of Solano, ultimately encompassing hundreds of families. Despite remaining autonomous from political parties and trade unions, they did, at different times, join different political alliances and coordinating bodies, most importantly the *Coordinadora de Trabajadores Desocupados Aníbal Verón* (Aníbal Verón Unemployed Workers' Coordination), which brought together many of the different autonomous unemployed workers' organizations to organize actions together and support one another's initiatives.

While the workshops focused on the specific experiences of the MTD of Solano, the complex cartography of different organizations of the unemployed is referenced throughout the book. Frequent mentions are made of organizations such as the *Federación Tierra y Vivienda* (Land and Work Federation, FTV, led by

---

1   Throughout the text, we use the gender-neutral term *piqueterxs,* taken up widely in recent years thanks to the mass feminist movement. It highlights the important role that women played in the movement as a whole, although it was often not recognized at the time. We opt to maintain the Spanish term rather than simply refer to "the unemployed," because, as the MTD of Solano explains later in this book, *piqueterx* refers to a political identity, an identity based on action and resistance, while "the unemployed" merely refers to a sociological description, and is often depoliticized and cast in the position of a victim.

Luis d'Elía) linked to the Central de Trabajadores Argentinos (Argentine Workers' Central Union, CTA), the *Corriente Clasista y Combativa* (Class-based and Combative Current, CCC, affiliated with the Revolutionary Communist Party), the *Polo Obrero* (Workers' Pole, affiliated with the Workers' Party) and the *Movimiento Teresa Rodríguez* (Teresa Rodríguez Movement, MTR). Each of these organizations have their own histories, compositions, practices, and ideological and theoretical positions. It is in that sense that Colectivo Situaciones refers to the unemployed workers' organizations as a whole as "a movement of movements." These different organizations and movements would sometimes come together in specific actions or campaigns. For example, a couple of "National Piquetero Congresses" attempted to bring together organizations of the unemployed across this spectrum, however, without much lasting success. As the MTD of Solano recounts here, there were major differences in terms of how to relate to the state and forms of internal organization. For the MTD of Solano, many of these other groups represent ways of doing politics based on a way of thinking based on "globality," thinking in terms of predefined concepts and understandings of power, rather than starting from the situation. That way of thinking, starting from the situation and insisting on the autonomy to define one's own concepts and on the self-affirmation of one's own project, is what sets the MTD of Solano apart from many of these other organizations of the unemployed.

Another major source of differences and tensions among the organizations of the unemployed was their relationship to "subsidies," the complex array of welfare benefits packages offered to the poor and the unemployed. These subsidies were one of the primary demands of the movements in the roadblocks and other mobilizations. Eventually, the demands included a wide range of programs offered by different levels of government (from municipalities to the federal government). Originally proposed as individual welfare benefits to the poor and the unemployed, the movements demanded, and won, the right to collectively administer the programs. This meant that organizations would receive the money, distribute it to their members, deciding who was eligible based on their own criteria and, if there where corresponding work requirements, determine what counted as "work" in order to receive benefits. Of course, this had mixed consequences. It led to a swelling of the ranks of the organizations of the unemployed, as people signed up in order to have access to those benefits. It also led to accusations of clientelism, of organizations essentially paying people to show up to their events or otherwise using the programs to the sole benefit of leaders. In other cases, it led to interesting experiments in collectivizing the benefits – pooling benefits to use them for common projects – and redefining what was considered work – valuing care and community labor above all else.

Of course, the organizations of the unemployed were also part of a broader constellation of movements, organizations, and alternative economic practices during the crisis. These include the neighborhood assemblies of largely middle-class urban neighborhoods and the barter clubs which extended across the country, using alternative currencies and barter to trade for goods and services as the official economy collapsed. As members of the MTD of Solano explain here, the movements of the unemployed had complicated and evolving relations with these other movements and practices, sometimes coming together across class differences and sometimes entering into irresolvable tension. Yet, as a whole, this complex constellation of movements was responsible for a unique moment of experimentation in terms of forms of life, ways of organizing economic and social relations, and of producing knowledge.

Twenty Years of 2001

A lot has changed in the two decades since *Hipotesis 891* was originally published. Ultimately, much of the energy of the 2001 revolt was institutionalized, with the election of Nestor Kirchner in 2003 and then of Cristina Fernández de Kirchner in 2007. Their administrations not only increased the subsidies and other benefit packages available to the poor, and specifically to social movements and cooperatives, but also incorporated movement leaders into government positions and created programs directly designed to booster those alternative economic activities that had emerged in the crisis. The conversations with the MTD of Solano included in this book make it clear that there were already intense debates about the issue of institutionalization between different organizations of the unemployed. These tensions only increased Kirchner's election as many organizations jumped on the opportunity to participate in official policies, while others began defining themselves precisely in opposition to that institutionalization and organized around explicitly fighting against the Kirchner governments, accusing them of co-opting and pacifying movements.

The position of the MTD of Solano can best be described in Raquel Gutierrez's terms as non-state-centric. In Gutiérrez's words, a non-state-centric politics "does not propose confrontation with the state as the central issue, nor is it guided by building strategies for its 'occupation' or 'takeover;' but rather, it is strengthened by defense of the common, it displaces the state and capital's capacity for command and imposition, and it pluralizes and amplifies multiple social capabilities for intervention and decision-making over public matters: it disperses power as it enables the reappropriation of collective decision-making and speech over matters that belong to everyone because they affect us all."[2] In that sense, the MTD of Solano always prioritized its own project: the project of creating new forms of life, new social relations, and new subjectivities in the neighborhoods where they worked. This never meant completely ignoring the realm of the state, and it often meant directly organizing forms of collective self-defense against state repression. Yet, they also continued occasionally receiving subsidies and grants from the state and other institutions, when they determined that doing so would further their organizational needs and not greatly sacrifice their autonomy. Most of members' energy went into the group's productive projects, from a bakery to community garden, their neighborhood health clinic, and popular education and pedagogical processes, and to maintaining the alliances and coalitions to support those projects. The MTD of Solano discusses this in terms of not letting their practice be defined by "the political conjuncture." Instead, the organization's project and needs, the project of creating new modes of life, were always prioritized over conflicts taking place at the level of state politics, no matter who was in the presidency.

The divisions which became present under Kirchner and Fernandez's governments, in some sense, only intensified with the election of right-wing neoliberal Mauricio Macri in 2015. Macri represented a return to many of the neoliberal economic policies of the 1990s, but with a friendlier face that sought to incorporate the popular sectors into the neoliberal project. In this sense, he sought to reestablish a neoliberal subjectivity at the base of society, individualizing welfare benefits and encouraging "entrepreneurship" at all levels of society.[3] Macri's administration was also responsible for taking out the largest IMF loan in the institution's history, for cutting subsidies for utilities for the middle class, and undercutting unions in wage negotiations. In this context, many movements became further entrapped by the spatialities and temporalities of state politics, focusing their energy on electoral campaigns and influencing politicians in power, rather than the autonomous grassroots experiments that had characterized much of the 2001 uprising.

It was also a period of new alliances and political strategies. Starting during Fernandez's government, Colectivo Situaciones and the MTD of Solano focused much of their efforts on constructing new alliances and research initiatives with

---

2   Raquel Gutiérrez Aguilar, *Horizonte Comunitario-Popular. Antagonismo y producción de lo común en América Latina.* (Cochabamba: Sociedad Comunitaria de Estudios Estratégicas y Editorial Autodeterminación, 2015), 89.

3   For more on these shifts in subjectivity and the spread of a "neoliberalism from below" during both the late Kirchner period and the Macri's government, see Verónica Gago's *Neoliberalism from Below: Popular Pragmatics and Baroque Economies* (Durham, NC: Duke Press, 2017) and Diego Sztulwark's *La ofensiva sensible: Neoliberalismo, populismo y el reverso de lo político* (Buenos Aires: Caja Negra, 2019).

emerging subjectivities of struggle, particularly migrants, precarious workers, and, later, feminist organizations and collectives. This research also focused on shifts at the level of popular subjectivity – on forms of what some referred to as microfascisms – as increased competition, identitarianism, and authoritarian behavior were being enacted on the extremely local level. One of the best examples of this was the case of Parque Indoamericano, in which three thousand families, mostly Bolivian and Paraguayan migrants, occupied the park and set up a temporary encampment, only to be violently attacked by middle class neighborhood residents and state forces. Three migrants were killed in the police's raid on the park celebrated by many of the white middle- and upper-class sectors of society.[4] Members of Colectivo Situaciones and the MTD of Solano worked together with collectives of migrants and other urban researchers in the *Hacer Ciudad* (Making the City) workshop to investigate changes occurring in the city, and the subjectivities of its inhabitants, at multiple scales. This research, and the network of alliances that carried out it, was thus able to diagnose the Macri government in a novel way, emphasizing those shifts in subjectivity that accompanied a generalized precarization of life.

Following years of organizing as the MTD of Solano, the organization eventually disbanded into a set of other smaller organizations working on particular projects, such as a community garden, a housing cooperative, and a health clinic. Those projects all maintain the original spirit of the MTD, an emphasis on struggle as the creation of new forms of life and new ways of living together. They also expanded their alliances, further developing their work with the Campesino Movement of Santiago de Estero (MOCASE), as well as building new collaborations with feminist and Indigenous movements. Similarly, Colectivo Situaciones disbanded as a collective around the same time, although its members continue to engage in other collective militant investigation processes.[5] These processes all keep the spirit of 2001 alive, emphasizing politics as creation and becoming, as questioning and uncertainty, of collective rebellion and resistance to institutionalization, as Colectivo Situaciones put it in 2010.[6]

---

4   For a militant research process analyzing the Parque Indoamericano Case, in which Colectivo Situaciones was involved with migrant collectives, see Taller Hacer Ciudad, *Vecinocracia: (Re)tomando la ciudad* (Buenos Aires: Tinta Limón and Editorial Retazos, 2011).

5   Much of this work can be seen on the blog Lobo Suelto (https://lobosuelto.com), in Verónica Gago's work with Ni Una Menos and other feminist collectives, in Mario Santucho's work with the magazine *Crisis* (https://revistacrisis.com.ar/), and Diego Sztulwark's work with various collectives, some of which is summarized in his book *La ofensiva sensible*. Furthermore, many of the collective's former members continue to be involved in the radical publishing house Tinta Limón.

6   "2001 does not refer to a year, but to an active principle, an interpretive key for understanding

Living in Freedom: Resonances Today

Twenty years after its original publication, the debates and themes raised in *Hipotesis 891* are more relevant than ever. Both the process from which the book emerged – research militancy – and the proposed concepts, such as counter-power, autonomy, horizontality, new forms of militant commitment, and new understandings of freedom, offer important insights for movements today. With this translation, we hope to contribute to the further circulation and dispersion of ideas and concepts, allowing them to travel to new territories, be transformed in the process, and contribute to the mutual contamination of struggles for our collective liberation.[7]

The first of these themes, and that which popularized Colectivo in the English-speaking world, is that of militant research or research militancy. The idea moved through different militant translations of Colectivo Situaciones' work and their participation in movement encounters and events across Europe and North America, entering into dialogue with other concepts ranging from *conricerca* to participatory-action research. *Hipotesis 891* does not offer theories of militant research, but rather demonstrates the process of militant research. As Colectivo Situaciones explain in the prologue, they understand militant research as both a critique of traditional forms of academic research, as well as the politics of most leftist movements and non-governmental organizations that is based on already knowing the answers. Instead, the offer a politics that in itself involves research, questioning, and collectively constructing responses. Colectivo Situaciones maintain a commitment to the knowledge produced in struggle and also a commitment to the idea that knowledge can and must be used for struggle. Today, when the term "militant research" is regularly used in academic articles and texts, it is worth returning to the question of the purpose and practice of research militancy. Ultimately, as *Hipotesis 891* highlights, research militancy is not primarily about another way of doing research, or least research that assumes academia as its main site of enunciation. Rather, it is about another way of doing politics, that does not follow a predetermined line or presume to know the answers a priori, but that sees research as part of the political process itself.

---

this decade" read the invitation to a series of events, organized by Colectivo Situaciones and friends to celebrate and interrogate the ten-year anniversary of the events of the 19th and 20th of December, 2001. The invitation continued: "For us, 2001 is almost a method, a way of looking at things seeing them in motion. In this sense the crisis becomes a premise, with its multiple meanings: instability and creation, worry and uncertainty, opening and changing the calendar."

7   For more on dispersion and the work of the book, as it travels, in the construction of movements and struggles, see Magalí Rabasa, *The Book in Movement: Autonomous Politics and the Lettered City Underground* (Pittsburgh, PA: University of Pittsburgh Press, 2019).

Another key theme, which highlights the uniqueness of the MTD of Solano's approach to politics and organizing, is their emphasis on the production of subjectivity. This emphasis highlights the fact that we are not fully formed subjects at the beginning of a political project and that politics takes place, among other levels, on the level of subjectivity. We see this emerge in two different ways in the MTD of Solano's analysis here. First, it can be seen in their critique of capitalism as producing particular subjectivities and desires, particularly as they see that manifest in their neighborhoods in terms of cut throat competition and lack of solidarity between neighbors. Rather than condemn those neighbors, they seek to understand how those elements are a fundamental part of capitalism's reproduction and expansion. The second element, involves asking how can the movement function as a space for the production of different subjectivities. Thus, they ask what pedagogical practices are necessary and what forms of decision-making and internal discussion are helpful for creating subjectivities that are not shaped by the logic of capitalism. Again, there is no predefined path for this, but it involves transforming all of those who participate in the project. As members of the MTD of Solano put it: "we have also proposed to recreate ourselves, to subject ourselves to change as well, as we have thrown all our certainties out the window." This also means willing to engage with comrades who make mistakes, recognizing how we all internalize elements of capitalist logic, and that we must be willing to work through the process of transformation together. Thus, instead of searching for the "right" subject to engage in revolutionary activity, whether determined by some sort of identity or class position, the MTD of Solano always understood their task to be that of producing a revolutionary subject.

Finally, the MTD of Solano always stood out, even in Argentina, for its understanding of power – and counter-power – and autonomy, moving beyond a state-centric politics. Counter-power, as posed by the MTD of Solano, is not in symmetrical opposition to power, the power of the state, the power of domination, power over. Rather, counter-power operates differently, on a different realm. Counter-power is the power of creation, the power to act, the power to affect and be affected by others. This commitment to counter-power lies at the heart of the MTD of Solano's non-state-centric politics, which is not driven by a logic of confrontation with the state nor the desire to take state power. Here autonomy arises as a *horizon*; not a fixed state, but a process through which and toward which the movement works. They attempt to progressively create more autonomy – both in terms of the sustainability of their alternative economic projects that allow them to meet some part of their daily needs while relying increasingly less on state subsidies, and in terms of the autonomy of thought and language, proposing their own analyses, their own concepts, for understanding and creating a world in which they would want to live in. Counter-power ultimately manifests itself in enacting other ways of living together, ways of organizing work without bosses and managers, ways of living together beyond the model of heterosexual nuclear family, ways of co-inhabiting spaces without hierarchical control. Or as the MTD proposes, "It is very important to recognize that it is not about transforming the municipal government, or the police force, among other things, but rather that these things exist today as things that we no longer want, we reject them, we negate them. We don't want to substitute any part of that system; we want to build something different. And it is that new thing that we are envisioning, constructing. That is counter-power." This is a project that ultimately proposes "a project of living in freedom," understood as freedom from capitalist imperatives of how to live our lives and the collective creation of new forms of life that allow us to fully live and relate to one another.

Liz Mason-Deese
Newport, VA
November 2021

Initial Words

To those who came before

This book emerged in the form of a dialogue between the Unemployed Workers' Movement (MTD) of Solano and Colectivo Situaciones. The encounter and the writing in common constitute a unique experience for all those who participated. In the following pages, the reader will not find – we think – an ordinary relationship between "activist" or "militants" and "committed intellectuals," nor any other standardized forms of understanding this experience of thinking in common that, as such, decodes and un-defines the being of each of us who has participated in these encounters.

The first part of this book is composed of conversations, in their entirety, that appeared at the beginning of 2001 in the pamphlet *Situaciones 4*, now preceded by an introduction that outlines the *motives and reasons* behind the project that we started three years ago. These are followed by two texts, or "working papers," that transcribe two workshop-meetings in terms of their internal and everyday dynamics.

In the second part, we reproduce three texts (the first was drafted by Colectivo Situaciones for the workshop, and the other two are part of the MTD of Solano's reflections on the events that took place in December 2001) published in the book *19th and 20th: Notes for a New Social Protagonism.*

In the third part, we present the development of conversations that took place between June 26, 2002 (the date of the massacre on the Pueyrredón Bridge) and mid-October, when the first edition was published: the themes, as well as the emphasis, continue to change. The introduction to this final last part – published here for the first time – is a brief reflection about the events that took place on June 26, followed by a set of twelve hypotheses, which were elaborated on during workshops that took place throughout this project. The extensive conversations in this third part, concluding the center of this book, are followed by two texts about the ending: an epilogue written by the MTD of Solano, and an annex about the encounter that took place on the first Sunday in October during John Holloway's visit to Solano.

Hypothesis 891 is the title of this book. All those who took part in this project chose this title together. The reasons for this are simple: the book tries to bring together two essential components of our experience: on the one hand, the unfinished – hypothetical – character of radical thought; and on the other, the number that indicates the *site* where these thoughts were produced, that as such resists all labeling and has functioned as a home, against all the dogmatism, academicism, and definitive "recipes."

Hypothesis 891 was only possible because neighborhood assemblies organized in the MTD Solano wanted it to happen. As noted somewhere in this book, the comrades from the MTD who participated in the project did so through the will expressed in the neighborhood assemblies. It is essential not to lose sight of how much this book belongs to them. We thank our comrades Chapa and Flor for their ongoing collaboration, Cucho for his time and design, and Raúl Zibechi for his continuous suggestions and dialogue.

On Method

I

Is a prologue internal or external to the text that it precedes? As we know, the prologue precedes from the end: although it opens the book, it is the last part to be written. It is not, then, a text that is internal to the book, nor is it completely external to it. It is, rather, both at the same time. It is external; yes, it is "post." It speaks from "after" the book's closing. It is a "second closure" that opens. But this new beginning – *starting afterward* – makes the main body of the text exist in another way: as if by being prefaced, it was *projected* and *prolonged*.

This extension is not a mere continuation, but rather an operation that reveals a form of work. This book is always already a *prolongation*: the prolongation of an encounter in a workshop, of one workshop into many others, of those workshops into an initial publication, that of the original dossier (*Situaciones 4; Conversations with the MTD of Solano*), from the dossier – already re-edited and out of print again – into this book that, in turn, will itself be prolonged in its readers, and becomes available for many other possible prolongations. [We might add that it is again prolonged, temporally, linguistically, geographically, in its translation many years later.]

The names of its authors – the Movimiento de Trabajaodores Desocupados (MTD) [Unemployed Workers' Movement] of Solano and Colectivo Situaciones – could, somehow, appear excessive. This became clear to us when we wanted to legally register the publication. For the state institutions in charge of regulating and registering everything that has the shape of a book – be it anything capable of adopting this form – the *author* is a fact whose absence cannot be excused. If for any reason this *name* were not available, one would have to resort to a pseudonym (which always names the responsible person, either the *author* or the *editor*). One way or the other, the *author* must appear; someone must take responsibility for what *is* said.

We do not believe that we are incredibly original by reminding the reader that the "author" – *authorship*, from *authority* – has died. This book will therefore be what other forces, other becomings, are capable of doing with it. The death of the author is not only a fashionable phrase, it also has concrete implications: it means that our intention as "authors" is not what counts here, that authorship is just a resource, an element, an item that is not worth spending time on.

This prologue, therefore, does not intend to promote a certain "appropriate" reading of the text – although, inevitably, it does suggest perspectives – nor does it anticipate conclusions that would be "suitable" to the intentions of those of us who participated in its making. Here prolongation does not mean the restriction of possible readings, but precisely the opposite: an offering, the act of delivering an object – that condenses encounters, thoughts – to the forces of new encounters and thoughts. [Similarly, this translation – one of many, and one that arises from specific encounters between the translators and the authors – does not purport to be the only possible translation but an opening up to many new translations and encounters.]

Therefore, there is no "author," but there *is* a work composed of rhythms, passions, forces, inspirations, thoughts, and affects. Those demand prolongations and epilogues. Those believe they can reveal something about themselves in what follows, while at the same time adding some clues about the figure of the *research militant* – an approximate word game to name the precarious existential equilibrium of a new form of commitment.

II

Militant research, as we understand it, lacks an *object*. We are aware of the *paradoxical* nature of this statement – if one does research, one performs research on *something;* if there is nothing to research, how can we talk about research? – and, at the same time, we are convinced that it is exactly this nature that gives militant research its *potencia*.[8] To investigate without objectifying, implies abandoning the conventional image of the researcher. And that is what the *militant researcher* aspires to do.

In fact, research can be a road to *objectification* (again, we are not being original by confirming this old knowledge, and, yet, this effect is one of the most serious

---

8   In Spanish, there are two words for "power": "poder" and "potencia," which derive from the Latin words "potestas" and "potentia." Colectivo Situaciones' understands power based on this distinction they take from Spinoza. While "potencia" has a dynamic, constituent dimension, "poder" is static, constituted. *Potencia* defines our power to do, to affect, and be affected, while the mechanism of representation that constitutes "poder" separates "potencia" from the bodies that are being represented. To preserve the emphasis of this distinction, the Spanish word "potencia" is used, where appropriate, throughout this book. – Trans.

limitations of the usual subjectivity of the researcher). As Nietzsche reminds us, theoretical man (and woman) – which is something more complex than "the man (and woman) who reads" – is the one who perceives action from an entirely external point of view (that is to say, their subjectivity is constituted in a way that is completely independent with respect to that action). In this way, the theorist works by *attributing* an intention to the subject of the action. Let's be clear: every attribution of this kind supposes, in relation to the protagonist of the observed action, an *author* and an *intention*; confers values and goals, and, in the end, produces "knowledge" *about* the action (and the actor).

Following this path, critical activity remains oblivious in regards to at least two essential moments. On the one hand, concerning the – external – *subject* who exercises the critique. Researchers do not need to investigate themselves. They can construct consistent knowledge *about* the situation to the extent – and, precisely, due to the fact – that they remain on the *outside*, at the prudent distance that, supposedly, guarantees a certain *objectivity*. And yes, this objectivity is authentic and efficacious to the same extent that it is nothing but the other side of the coin of the objectification – *violence* – of the situation *on* which the researcher works. [Meanwhile, the translator translates "neutrally" and "objectively," always from a *double outside*.]

But there is yet a second aspect in which critical activity remains oblivious: the researcher – in their act of *attribution* – does nothing but adapt the *resources* that are available at the situation of their investigation to the unknowns presented by the object. The researcher, in this way, constitutes themselves into a machine that confers meanings, values, interests, kinships, causes, influences, rationalities, intentions, and unconscious motives to their object.

Both blind spots, or perhaps the same blind spot in regards to two issues (concerning the *subject who attributes* and concerning the *resources of attribution*), come together in the configuration of a *single* operation: a machine that judges *good* and *evil* according to the set of *available values*.

This modality of knowledge production presents us with a clear dilemma. Traditional academic research – with its *object*, its *method* of attribution, and its *conclusions* – obtains, of course, valuable knowledge – that is mostly descriptive – in regard to the *objects* it investigates. But this descriptive operation in no way occurs after the object's formation, because it itself produces that objectification. Thus, academic research is much more effective when it best uses these objectifying powers. Thus, *science* operates much more as separation – and reification – of the situations in which it participates than as an internal element in the creation of (both practical and theoretical) possible experiences.

The researcher offers themselves as a subject of the *synthesis* of the experience. The researcher is the one who explains the rationality of what happens, and is preserved as such: as a necessary blind spot of that synthesis. The researcher, as the subject who *gives meaning,* remains exempted from any self-examination. That researcher and their resources – their values, their notions, their gaze – constitute themselves into the machine that classifies, gives coherence, inscribes, judges, discards and excommunicates. In the end, it is the intellectual who "does justice" regarding matters of *truth*, in terms of the administration – or adequacy – of what exists under the present horizon of rationality.

III

We have mentioned *commitment* and *militancy*. Are we perhaps proposing the superiority of the *political militant* in opposition to the academic researcher?

We do not believe so. Political activism is also a practice with an object. As such, it has remained tied to a mode of instrumentality: one that connects to other experiences from an always already constituted subjectivity, with prior knowledge – the knowledges of *strategy* –, supplied with universally valid, purely ideological statements. It relates to others through *utilitarianism*: there is never *affinity*, always "agreement," never encounter, always "tactics." Political activism – especially that of the political party – can hardly constitute itself into an experience of *authenticity.* From the very beginning it gets stuck in *transitivity:* what it finds interesting in an experience is always "something other" than the experience itself. From this point of view, political militancy – and militants on the Left are no exception – is as external, judgmental, and objectifying as university research.

Let's add the fact that the humanitarian activist – let's say from an NGO – does not escape these manipulative mechanisms. Strictly speaking, the now globalized humanitarian ideology is constituted from an idealized image of *an already made, unchangeable world.* Faced with that world, the only remaining possibility is to dedicate efforts to those – more or less *exceptional* – places where misery and irrationality still reign.

Not only do the mechanisms unleashed by humanitarian solidarity foreclose any possible creation, but they also naturalize – with the compassionate resources of beneficence and their language about *exclusion* – the victimizing objectification that separates each person from their subjective and productive possibilities. [While the *humanitarian translator* makes sure that those poor victims voices are heard, translated into the language of those with power.]

If we refer to the commitment and the "militant" character of research, we do so in a precise sense, connected to four conditions: a) the motive underpinning research; b) the practical character of research (elaboration of practical situated hypotheses); c) the value of what is being investigated: the result of research can only be evaluated in its totality in situations that share the problematics being investigated, as well as the constellation of conditions and concerns; and d) its effective procedure: its process of development is already a result in and of itself, and its results lead to an immediate intensification of effective procedures.

IV

In fact, every *idealization* strengthens this mechanism of objectification. This is an authentic problem for the militancy of research. Idealization – even when it falls on an object not consecrated to such effect – always results from a mechanism of attribution (even when it does not happen under the pretext of scientific or political pretensions). Because idealization – like any ideologization – expels everything from the constructed *image* that could cause it to lose its status as an *ideal* of coherence and completeness.

What happens, however, is that every ideal – contrary to what the idealist believes – is more on the side of death than on that of life. The ideal cuts reality off from life. The concrete – the living – is partial and irremediably inconceivable, incoherent, and contradictory. The *living* – to the extent that it persists in its capacities and *potencias* – does not need to adjust itself to an image that gives it meaning or justifies it. It is the other way around – living is in itself a creative source – not an object or repository – of values of justice. In fact, the entire idea of a *pure* or *complete* subject is nothing but the conservation of this *ideal*.

Idealization conceals an operation that is inadvertently conservative: behind the purity and vocation for justice that seem to be its origin, its foundation in dominant values is once again hidden. Thus, the righteous appearance of the idealist: they want to do justice, in other words, their desire is to materialize, to make effective, the values that they hold as good. Idealists do nothing but project these values onto the idealized (this is the moment when what was multiple and complex turns into an *object*, corresponding to an ideal) without asking themselves about their own values; more importantly, without undergoing a subjective *experience* that transforms themselves.

This mechanism reveals itself as the most serious of obstacles for the militant researcher. Originating in subtle and almost unperceivable forms, idealization slowly produces an almost *unbridgable chasm*. To the extent that the militant researcher only manages to see their own projections on what appears to them as already complete.

That is why this activity cannot exist unless a very serious work *on* the research *collective* itself takes place; in other words, it cannot exist without doing serious research on itself, without changing itself, without reconfiguring itself through the experiences in which it takes part, without revising the ideals and values it holds dear, without constantly criticizing its own ideas and understandings, and in the end, without developing practices that expand in all possible directions.

This ethical dimension points to the complexity of militant research: the subjectifying work of deconstructing every inclination towards objectification. In other words: carrying out research without an object.

Like in *genealogy*, it is all about working at the level of the *"criticism of values."* It is about penetrating and destroying "its statues," as Nietzsche affirms. But this work that is oriented by – and towards – the *creation of values* is not done by mere "contemplation." It requires a radical critique of the prevailing values. That is why it involves an effort to *deconstruct* the dominant forms of perception (*interpretation, valorization*). Therefore, there is no creation of values without the production of a subjectivity capable of submitting itself to a radical critique.

V

One question becomes clear: is such an investigation possible without at the same time setting in motion a process of *falling in love*? How would the link between two experiences be possible without a strong feeling of *love* or *friendship*?

In fact, the experience of militant research resembles that of a person in love, on the condition that by *love* we understand what a certain long – materialist – philosophical tradition understands by it: that is, not as something that happens to someone in relation to the other, but a process that *takes* two or more; a process that transforms the "self" into the "common." One *participates* in such a relationship of love. Such a process is not decided intellectually: it *takes* the existence of two or more. It is not an illusion, but an authentic experience of anti-utilitarianism.

In love, in friendship, contrary to the mechanisms we describe above, there is neither objectivity nor instrumentalism. Nobody is spared from what the bond *can* do, nobody comes out from it uncontaminated. One does not experience love or friendship in an innocent way: we all leave them reconstituted. These *potencias* – love and friendship – have the power to constitute, qualify, and remake the subjects they catch. [And the translator, how could they not fall in love, how could they not be remade in the process of translating a text such as this? That is what makes translation an *act of love*.]

This love – or friendship – is constituted as a relationship that renders undefined what until that moment was preserved as individuality, composing an integrated figure made up of more than one individual body. And, at the same time, such a qualification of the individual bodies participating in this relationship causes the failure of all the mechanisms of abstraction – *dispositifs* that turn bodies into quantifiable, interchangeable objects – as characteristic of the capitalist market as the other mechanisms of objectification we have mentioned.

Thus, we consider this *love* a condition of militant research.

In this book we refer several times to these processes of friendship or *falling in love*, under the – less compromising – name of *composition*. Different from *articulation*, *composition* is not merely intellectual. It is neither based in interests nor in criteria of (political or another type of) convenience. In contrast to (strategic or tactic, partial or total) "agreements" or "alliances" founded on coincidences expressed in a text, composition is more or less inexplicable, and goes beyond everything one can say about it. In fact – at least while it lasts – it is much more intense than any merely political or ideological compromise.

Love and friendship tell us about the value of quality over quantity: the power of the collective body composed of other bodies does not increase according to the mere quantity of its individual components, but in relation to the *intensity* of the bond that unites them.

VI

Love and friendship, then: the work of research militancy is not to be identified with the production of a party line. It works – necessarily – on another plane.

If we sustain the distinction – as we try to throughout this book – between "politics" (understood as the battle for power) and the experiences in which processes of the production of sociability or values are at stake, we can distinguish then between the political militant (who founds their discourse on a certain set of certainties) and the militant researcher (who organizes their perspective on the basis of critical questions concerning these certainties).

Yet, this distinction is often lost from sight, in the belief that what can be seen in the experience of the MTD of Solano – particularly following the *Situaciones 4* pamphlet – is just one more party line.

In some way, then, some have thought they have seen the birth of a "situationist" line, as an idealized product of language – or even the *jargon* – of the publication and the image that – apparently – the pamphlet transmits – at least in some readings – of the experience.

Detractors and adherents to this new line have created a motive for disputes and conspiracies out of it. In this regard, all we can do is admit that out of all the possible outcomes of this encounter, these *reactions* are the ones that motivate us the least, both because of the manifest improducitivity that results from such repudiation and adhesion and because of how such idealizations (whether positive or negative) usually replace a more critical vision about those making them. Thus, a too closed position is rapidly adopted out of what is supposed to be an exercise of opening.

We have already admitted that we cannot control *interpretations*. But perhaps we did not think about a particular implication of this point of view. The death of the author turns the *reader* into the subject responsible for creating a meaning based on the text. And in this very operation, the reader-author is *produced* (one who does not preexist and will not endure beyond what they can do with the text). Thus, the supposed original author has lost their right to tell the reader what to do with their reading. What the "author" (as a *talking corpse*) can indeed do is read the understandings that have been made of their texts; in other words, intervene as reader. It is only in this character that we pronounce ourselves decidedly in open refusal of the *purely political* interpretation of the present text.

VII

Let's take another step in constructing the concept of research *without* an object. *Interiority* and *immanence* are not necessarily identical processes.

Inside and *outside*, *inclusion* and *exclusion*, are categories of the *dominant ideology* (if we are allowed such an expression): they usually hide more than they reveal. That is, the experience of militant research is not one of being *inside*, but of working from *immanence*.

Let's say that the difference can be presented in the following terms: the *inside* (and therefore the *outside*) defines a position organized *from* a certain *boundary* that is considered *relevant*. Inside and outside refer to the location of a body or element in relation to a disjunction or a border. To be inside is also – in this line – to share a common property, which makes us belong to a same *set*.

This system of references interrogates us about the place where we are *situated*: nationality, social class, or even the site where we choose to *situate* ourselves in regards to... the next elections, the military invasion of Colombia or cable television programming...

In the extreme, both "objective" *belonging* (that derives from the *observation* of a common property) and "subjective" *belonging* (that derives from *choice* in the face of) come together to the joy of the social sciences: if we *are* unemployed workers we can *choose* to join a *piqueterx* movement; if we are from the middle class we can *choose* to be part of a neighborhood assembly. Through *determination* – collective belonging to the same group, in this case social class – choice (the group of commons with which we will join) becomes possible – and desirable –.

In both cases *being inside* implies respecting a pre-existing boundary that distributes places and belonging in a more or less involuntary way. It is not about denying the possibilities that derive from the moment of choice – which can be, as in the case of these examples, highly subjectifying, but distinguishing the mere "being" and its "inside" (or "*outside,*" it does not matter), from the mechanisms of subjective production that arise from disobeying those destinies. At the border, it is not as much about reacting in the face of already codified options as it is about producing the terms of the situation ourselves.

In this sense it is worth presenting the image of *immanence* as something other than merely *being inside*.

Immanence refers to a mode of *inhabiting* the *situation* and works from *composition* – love or friendship – in order to bring about new possible elements of this situation. Immanence is constituent co-belonging that traverses the representations of "inside" and "outside" transversally or diagonally. Where interiority demands a mode of being that is exhausted in belonging or adhesion, immanence implies inhabiting the experience, opening it to the possible *potencias* of composition. [Immanent translation expands this composition, in all directions at once, the translator is neither inside nor outside the situation, be actively composing, weaving, it together with new situations.]

Summing-up: *immanence, situation, composition* are notions that are internal to the experience of militant research. Useful names for the operations that organize a becoming common and, above all, *constituent.* If, in other experiences, they turn into the jargon of a new political line or categories of a fashionable philosophy – something that does not interest us at all – they will, for sure, obtain a new meaning based on those *uses* which are not ours.

In other words: the operational difference between the "inside" of representation (foundation of *belonging and identity*) and the *connection* of immanence (the *constituent* becoming) has to do with the greater *openness* that the latter form grants us for participating in new *experiences*.

VIII

It seems like we have arrived at the production of a difference between *love-friendship* and the forms of objectification against which the – precarious, we insist – figure of the militant researcher seeks to rebel.

Yet, we have not entered in the –fundamental – matter of the ideologization of confrontation.

Struggle activates capacities, resources, ideals, and solidarities. As such it speaks to us about a vital disposition, about dignity. In it, the risk of death is neither pursued nor desired. Thus, the meaning of the dead comrades will never be complete, but rather, painful. This dramatic quality of struggle is, however, made banal when the confrontation is put in ideological terms, to the point that they are postulated as its exclusive meaning.

When this happens there is no room for research. As we know, both – ideology and investigation – have opposite structures: while the first is constituted from a set of certainties, the second only exists on the basis of a grammar of questions.

Yet, struggle – the necessary, noble struggle – does not in itself lead to the exaltation of confrontation as the dominant meaning of life. There is no doubt that the limit can appear very thin in the case of an organization in permanent struggle, like a *piqueterx* organization, and yet, to give up on this point would be to prejudge.

Unlike the militant subjectivity that is usually sustained through a meaning given by the extreme polarization of life – the ideologization of confrontation –, the experiences that seek to construct another type of sociability are very active in trying not to fall into the *logic of confrontation*, according to which the multiplicity of experience is reduced to this dominant signifier.

Confrontation, on its own, does not *create values*. As such it does not go beyond the distribution of dominant values.

The result of a war shows us who will appropriate what exists. Who will have property rights over goods and existing values?

If struggle does not *alter* the "structure of meanings and values" we are only in the presence of a change of roles, which guarantees the survival of the structure itself.

Once we have arrived at this point, two completely different images of justice – because in the end that's what this is about – are sketched out before us. On one side, the struggle is for the ability to use the *judging machine*. To make justice is to claim for oneself what is considered just. It is to interpret the distribution of existing values in another way. The other image suggests that it is about becoming *creators* of values, of experiences, of worlds.

IX

This prologue affirms that the book it opens for us does not speak of a *model* experience. Moreover, it continues – insistently – to affirm that it is against the existence of such ideals. It will be said – and with reason – that it is one thing to utter this principle and something very different to achieve it in practice. One can also conclude – and here our doubts start – that in order for this noble purpose to become a reality it would be necessary for us to make "our criticisms" explicit (in this case, *Colectivo Situaciones'* criticisms of the *MTD of Solano*). If we were to look at this demand closely, we would see how it asks us to *save* the *model* – now in a negative way – by comparing the *real experience* to the *ideal model,* a mechanism that is used by the social sciences to extract their "critical judgments."

As we can see, all these reflections on criticism and the production of knowledge are not minor issues, and that is because they concern forms of justice (and judgment is nothing but the judicial form of justice). This book can offer nothing that resembles a juridical event, nor does it provide resources to make judgments about other experiences. Rather, the opposite is the case: if we have tried to do something as "authors" – talking corpses that write – it has been to offer an image that is completely opposed to juridical justice, or, in other words, a justice founded on *composition. What is it good for*? There are no predetermined answers.

C.S., October 17th 2002
[Translated, LMD, May 2020]

Motives and Reasons

Colectivo Situaciones

I

The Movement of Unemployed Workers (MTD) of Solano consists of eight hundred families from different neighborhoods in the locality, some of which include some settlements that have existed for over twenty years.[9] In August 1997, they started organizing themselves around the parish of San Martín and since then have multiple projects and experiments: their participation in the *piqueterx* movement was the best known of these. Our relationship with the MTD-S started a while ago. The first encounter, the first conversations, the first project, the first year of the project, and as a result of the growth of this bond, the first published pamphlet – *Situaciones 4: Conversations with the MTD Solano* – brings together all of what we collectively worked on throughout 2001. That pamphlet was published the first week of December, days before the actions that took place on 19th and 20th December. We have elaborated the first part of this book based on that original text.

II

The workshop was carried out between piles of tires and precarious little wooden benches, in a warehouse whose appearance now varies greatly from how it looked during those first meetings, it has been changing, growing.

Those first encounters – that now seem long ago – were frankly very *strange*.

---

9   Solano is a city in the Province of Buenos Aires (divided between the counties of Quilmes and Almirante Brown), in the city's urban periphery. It has some of the highest population density in the area, as well as highest rates of poverty, labour and housing precarity, police violence, and contamination and associated health risks. It has also long been a site of land takeovers and settlements by the organized poor. – Trans.

On the one hand, it was clear, at least to us, that we had found an experience with which we immediately felt connected. These feelings quickly grew until they turned into solid bonds. Nonetheless – and this is the other side – it took us a long time to figure out what this relationship consisted of, to be able to – concretely – respond to the question of "what are we doing here" with this uninterrupted and frequent regime of encounters.

This question takes on its full meaning when we observe that the bond that we were establishing was able, from the beginning, to escape from the traditional representations that normally structure the meaning of "socially motivated" encounters. This is what occurs with well-intentioned "solidarity" that is not able to move beyond a crude classism, unable to disassociate itself from the character of "involuntary excess" with which the powerful refer to the "excluded," thus producing their – objective, but also subjective – condition as victims.

For the cosmovision that "adores the poor," it is vital that such poverty correspond, at the same time, to an impoverishing subjective existence: the experience of mere survival. That is where this tone comes from, that tone that is so particular to a certain type of solidarity and does not question the very distribution of places established by the capitalist machine. This type of solidarity represents itself through images of the "winners" (those who have the luxury of solidarity) and "losers" (seen as animals, perceived as incapable of autonomous action and thought).

However, the birth of the – heterogeneous – *piqueterx* movement made a significant contribution toward altering this perception. That is what awakens political interest in the movement. As much for its impressive capacity to mobilize as for the radical nature of its methods of struggle, the *piqueterx* movement has been transformed into an authentic *object of desire* for revolutionary politics.

Nonetheless, this is not the most *interesting* thing about experiences such as that of the MTD Solano. Or at least, it is not for those of us who have been forewarned about how certain leftist *politics* construct their icons and are most concerned with identifying the concrete obstacles to experiences of counter-power – and with the thought and practices organized around them – than to fighting to gain adhesions to this or that revolutionary "program."

But the issue is that the *piqueterx* movement – with the help of the media and political discourse – presented itself as one homogeneous movement, until the moment when it was politically "divided" into ideologically distinct fractions.

This – sociologizing – view, nonetheless, hides the precariousness of such unity. Although dominant, this perception of one movement – "division" is clearly predicated on the existence of the "one" – does not allow for seeing of the singularity (multiplicity) of each of the local movements, in which different histories and trajectories develop and do not necessarily coincide – except in common situations that, contrary to what is believed, are very specific.

As such, what unites them is the same situation of social "marginality" – those "without work" – a certain immediate dependency in respect to the state – government benefits and subsidies – and the method of struggle – the roadblock. This is no small thing. Nonetheless, these "factors" do not *touch on* the *subjective materiality* of what happens within each movement.

In our case, our encounter with the MTD-S tended to make the idea of the existence of a "*piqueterx* movement" seem more and more abstract. Not because the common "factors" that we just mentioned do not exist, but because these factors are not subjectively organized in the same way for each movement, which makes the term "piqueterx" an overly homogeneous representation for speaking about a very diverse reality.

That is why here we prefer to refer to a single unique experience: that which we have known in Solano over the past few years.

We are not, therefore, simply, faced with a movement fighting for social justice. As if this were a "small" thing – and as if it could be – this part of the struggle does not fully encompass the experience of the MTD Solano. The light that emerges from the MTD Solano is fueled by an *excess* in respect to the demand for social equality: inquiry into the production of new values, a sociability that surpasses individualism.

A movement that functions as a shining light can very easily be confused with a "model" or a "line" of ideological thought and action. The *difference* can be so shallow that it is not worth *insisting* on it. Yet, the opposite is true: this *insistence* is a particularly important resource because it allows for *seeing* this *difference* between inquiry that "keeps open" precisely that which "the model" and "line" undoubtedly "close off" and "abstract."

III

What does this opening, the *potencia* of the MTD-S's intervention consist of? Even if there is no one answer to this question that, as such, depends excessively on the concerns that organize the question, what has drawn our interest is the fact that – and the form in which – the MTD-S has tackled the genuine conditions of social fragmentation to produce a fabric of solidarity and production from those conditions.

These are not abstract observations. By not assuming the position of the victim – an attitude of waiting, passivity, a discourse that is reduced to "necessities," etc. – the members of the MTD-S produce a new perspective – capacities and knowledge – whose effectiveness consists of empowering different (economic, political, cultural, artistic) projects among the neighborhood residents and families connected to the movement. Initially these were oriented toward resolving problems such as unemployment, nutrition, and education and training, but, at the same time – and this extra is essential – are able to produce social cohesion and multiply the various dimensions of existence (values and meanings).

This extra demonstrates the universality of the MTD-S's work, by working as a nucleus, knitting together sociability in a context where there is a radical dispersion of collective bodies. This point of view, clearly, connects the MTD-S's actions with other such experiences that combat the – material and spiritual – impoverishment of the existence of people and communities and emphasize the struggle against sadness, misery, and impotency starting in the movement itself.

The MTD-S thus intervenes both as a radically *singular* experience (as a subjective experience produced in conditions of extreme fragmentation) and on a *universal* plane (as part of a counter-power that establishes a situational sovereignty founded on the struggle against impotency) through a group of (diverse) projects based on strongly valuing autonomy, situated thought, and, as a counterpart, on a relative subtraction in respect to classical political knowledges.

It is these characteristics (horizontal forms of working together and making decisions, new types of connections and exchanges with other experiences) that give new meaning to the roadblocks and their way of associating with the State. At the same time, it is what does not allow for considering these "factors" as holding a pre-established meaning, other than that which is elaborated within the situation.

IV

In our societies, the *"excluded"* are spoken about; those who are "outside", those who have been "expelled". This is not simply referring to the "poor", which would only designate a quantitative (and perhaps even variable) difference in terms of resources, but a new social figure: one who "no longer belongs" (who no longer shares any habits, their conduct is unpredictable, their miserable norms of consumption and ways of acquiring food are absolutely incomprehensible). "Exclusion" is no longer a quantitative difference of resources, nor is it reversible. It presents itself as a border with barbarism that one must not cross, because, if you do, you will not return from this "no man's land," where neither the law nor language exist.

Nonetheless, despite being so kind as to name "that" which is on the other side of the imaginary barrier – beyond the desert – "exclusion" is a traditionally *ideological* category, in the sense that it hides much more than it reveals. Exclusion is the specific form in which our societies *include* – represent – the growing part of society that is *produced* – precisely – as "excluded," and is taken into account as such.

This is the success of this notion of "exclusion": it names what society itself produces *as if* it were not responsible for this production. On the one hand, it allows for hiding the hypocrisy with which the *"included"* regret this duality – washing their hands of all causal relations between one reality and another. On the other, it enables anyone to occupy a place within representations – again of the *included* and *excluded* – and thus give meaning to what would otherwise be the presence of an absolutely intolerable reality.

In effect, *produced* as such, *perceived* as such, and as a logical result of these operations, *treated* as such, the "excluded" – the *other* of inclusion – are "liberated" (in the same perverse and cynical sense in which the proletariat are "free" under capitalism, as a labor force that "voluntarily" agrees to their labor contract) from symbolic and juridical law. In effect, in the *desert* there is constant struggle.

The *potencia* of experiences like that of the MTD-S does not consist of – as the discourse of the excluded would state – the heroic deed of having organized the inhabitants of the desert, as made evident by their ability to build practices and declarations that are capable of destroying and moving beyond the binary pair of exclusion/inclusion.

While originally it was about "unemployed workers", that is, in the beginning they identified themselves based on a deficiency, a lack, which condemned them to the *desert*, their own development drove them to look for new ways of naming themselves in accordance with their initial subjective experience. The "piqueterxs" is one of these names, but others continue to emerge: "authentic work," "autonomous work," etc.

Now it is not a matter of wanting to "return to work," of demanding to be reintegrated into a segment of the rotten social structure, that can only – eventually – accept them in conditions that they have learnt to despise.

Neither included, nor excluded, rather beyond these representations: something new is being woven.

V

According to Pablo Picasso, we only look for something precisely when *something* has been found. In other words, if what one is looking for is entirely unknown, we would never recognize it if we were to "encounter it". The "encounter" is the first step: meeting with the desire to search, to investigate, to believe, to produce.

Nonetheless, the uncertainly of the "new" – that is always a reorganization of the old, to leave room for terms and meanings that emerge from this new reorganization – creates fears and objections: What is beyond? Why try to travel along roads on which there are no guarantees?

According to the "certainties" that we can supposedly count on, "political" work consists of confronting *fragmentation* (social fragmentation produced by *neoliberalism*), through the *hegemonic* capacity to organize – centralize – such fragmentation, from a coherency provided by those (*totalizing*) political resources that we rely on: consciousness (*ours*, and "the other's" lack of it), organization (the program, the party), and finally, by controlling the state apparatus.

Seen from *above*, the *dispersion* of struggles and *fragmentation* of communities and cultures is a desired effect (for capital and its powers): we are called to accept these processes as if they were "inevitable tendencies," destined by a god (it is the economy that actually occupies that place today), faced with which, resignation is the only possibility.

Seen from *below*, on the other hand, dispersion is experienced as an atmosphere, as a *condition*: it is confirmed that the social ground is fragmented and thus the question arises of how to produce something in that atmosphere.

Three answers appear in the face of fragmentation: one consists of reacting against it and trying to produce a "central alternative power" that reunifies (rearticulates) the chaos of the fragments. This perspective attempts to build a *universal discourse* that speaks in terms of "representing everyone".

A second response can be formulated by emphasizing the *part,* the fragment. It would try to affirm a particularity in order to then struggle against *all the others*, to obtain benefits. This politics speaks in the name of the fragment, and is reinforced in fragmented conditions.

The third response would consist in creating – in the mists of dispersion – consistent space-times that, in turn, tend – through their own force – to project themselves *transversally.* This transversal flux can only speak in its *own* name, but that name does not function as a *private* – individual or group – name, but rather as a way of naming expansive *potencias* composed of physical, affective, and mental organs.

It is a question of attitudes in the face of the *totality*: the production of an *abstract* universality, the production of the fragment that affirms particularity, and the production of a concrete universal that, in turn, is affirmed as a *singular* situation.

VI

Politics, we would say, no longer occurs through *politics*. Social inflections and the starting points for transformation, for the most part, do no go through (or necessarily originate from) the political sphere.

The political – the state, partisan – pertains to our societies more as a machine that *records* (misappropriating) the echoes of the ongoing transformations rather than as a site that produces these transformations.

The illusion of the political consists precisely in believing in oneself as a producer (able to control and direct) of those – or other – transformations.

Neoliberals and postmodernists believed that they could see the exhaustion of all struggles for justice and freedom in this apparent end of the *centrality of politics*. With the politician dead, politics dead: the defeat of the "seventies" experience, as they say, means the defeat of all projects of radical transformation.

The end of the centrality of "the political," nonetheless, can be understood more as the exhaustion of the efficiency of a politicized "metalanguage" of the social, than the end of social *interventions* and struggles themselves.

In effect, the *political* lens no longer provides us with operations that are able to perceive (*translate, synthesize, reduce)* the real multiplicity of existing meanings and practices.

Nonetheless, the *political* resists: like *lens* that almost cannot *see*, or a *metalanguage* that almost no longer accepts *translations*, its persistence produces a reductionist effect with respect to social phenomena, which no longer allows for perceiving – nor producing – from that space. One of the effects of such persistence, then, is the blockage of the transversality of a counter-power that requires more acute self-perception in order to insist on its own development.

But, what type of politics would be able to overcome that political blockage? This question immediately takes us to the unknown dimension. As such, our only option for responding to this question is to introduce hypotheses for interpreting the social field that would enable an understanding of the transformations taking place.

VII

Hypothesis, thought, and verification are the names of a different image of politics that no longer looks to exclusive "models" or central organizing cores. It does not try to take meaning away from politics in order to transfer that meaning to other structures, but rather, and more precisely, it tries to "depoliticize politics" in order to bring it a little closer to the multiplicity of *existences*.

Foucault would say that the intellectual has stopped being *universal* in order to become *specific*: the intellectual no longer speaks in the name of *universal values,* but rather in function of their own ability and situation. This transformation – from which we are still learning – gives rise to new modes of working with social *inflections*: neither historians, nor archaeologists, nor theorists, nor prophets of counter-power. It is a question of trying care for ways of co-constituting nuclei that are able to produce a perspective that comes from within the experiences of a new sociability, strengthening and creating bonds, knowledges, and working hypotheses.

VIII

A series of images were present in each encounter. Assemblies, capacity building, workshops, meetings, marches, interviews, roads, bridge and street blockades, encounters, coordination, neighborhoods, the unemployed, meetings with the authorities in charge, production, guitar sessions, planning, mate circles, press conferences, the chapel, tires, discussions, *piquetes*, masks, movements, are the words that weave together the experiences of the MTD Solano. Articulated, these fragments, these sketches, compose a freshness that we saw in our frequent visits last year. We would have to add to these reoccurring concepts, an enormous and disturbing "noisy band" of young people, dancing and singing "piqueteros, ¡fuck yeah!" People coming in and out, with problems and solutions of all kinds, and still the picture is not yet complete. Those who speak throughout this dialogue, members of the movement, are young people, with an amazing vitality, who often arrive to the workshop exhausted, after indescribably adventurous days. We worked hours in these conditions, well into the evening.

Few edits have been made to the extensive conversation we reproduce in what follows. All the, minimal, changes have been suggested by the comrades from the MTD-S. The complete conversation consisted of eight hours of tape, carried out over the course of several days. The themes discussed included: first, the history of the movement, the criteria that they use for organizing and working together, their relationship with other movements of the unemployed throughout the country, their relationship with the media, with groups that come to them with diverse proposals, their way of understanding politics, and, finally, their reflections on counter-power. In this first part, we have also included working papers that pick up on what was discussed in the workshop on June 12 and 16, 2001. To carry out this work, along with the workshop itself, we have participated in the movement's meetings, several of its activities and commission meetings.

The participation of the comrades from the MTD-S in this project was approved by an assembly of the movement and what is accomplished here, be it a lot or a little, is entirely dedicated to that assembly.

32

Conversations between Colectivo Situaciones and the MTD Solano

September to October 2001

1. Capitalism in Situation

We are not looking for your opinion about what happens at the general level of politics, what the media organizes as issues that everyone must have an opinion about. Instead, we are interested in your reflections about how the world is experienced; how do you all, specifically, live; the process that you have been developing. How do you define the problems? How do you discuss them?

The idea is to express the richness that we have experienced here.

To start the conversation, then, we want to say that, in order to capture the strength of this experience, we need to move away from the immediate and automatic anti-capitalist discourse that is very abstract, thinking in terms of slogans like: "we don't want them to pay the external debt," "when we take power, it will solve all the problems," or "we have to stop the government's structural adjustment policies." Because, although these are very important, they hide the fact that power functions through very concrete and intimate mechanisms, which are always situated, and it is this form of power that we have to address. Therefore, the first question is, how does capitalism exist here, how is it manifested, and how does it present itself?

When you all arrived, we were we just finishing a meeting with all the delegates from the different projects. In that meeting we discussed the projects' budgets, their forms of production, and their goals. Although the MTD deploys criteria of collectively building an alternative form of production, when it comes to defining things, capitalism is still very strong. As we know, it is very difficult to collectively build something using a capitalist mentality. Some of the obstacles we face include: individualism, selfishness, prioritizing solutions to personal problems over the interests of other comrades.

For example, it is very difficult to start producing when we have not yet established the purpose of what we are producing: if it will be to sell, or if it is for the common good, to create a collective economy based on solidarity.

Capitalism has managed to generalize an image or a projection of what constitutes happiness. To the extent that many people, even at the worst point of misery, never abandon the fantasy that one day they will be "saved." It is the idea of a lottery, of an individual salvation that is very much oriented towards a certain type of culture: that happiness is achieved by resolving the problem of housing, having a good car or the latest shoes. Capitalism developed this whole imaginary over the course of centuries. That is the hope, or the idea, in popular neighborhoods: that one day, they will be able to access what is being sold as happiness. Therefore, people like Susana Giménez[10] are hugely popular because they are part of the show business world. The popular sectors voted for Menem: he rode around in a Ferrari, rubbed elbows with the elites, and instead of being hated, he was admired because he was someone who "triumphed" in life.[11] This is one of the obstacles: there is an imaginary that is the result of centuries of domination. This idea of happiness is very ingrained.

Here in the neighborhoods, you can clearly see the destruction this has wreaked on individuals, on the community, on its values. Because, I think, capitalism has generated its own values, for example, that of "progress," of having certain status, of "being someone," as we often say. And being someone means having material things. That is how capitalism is experienced.

Even though there is a great deal of poverty here, there are many people in Solano who live based on those values. Even religion affirms that if you are good, if you behave well, you have a chance to get ahead. Many people are convinced that if you are not someone important, it is because you didn't study, you didn't try; in other words, this is reproduced in the form of guilt. Many people reach a certain age and feel like their life has been a total failure. All of this is related to individualism, which is where latent capitalist values are found.

---

10   A popular Argentine television host, actress, and model known for her right-wing views.
11   Carlos Menem, former president of Argentina (1989–1999), largely responsible for ushering in neoliberal structural adjustment policies.

We face constant tension in our organization as we try to put forth a project that speaks of the community, of a common effort, the idea that liberating ourselves is not about making ourselves rich, but rather that wealth and happiness are related to other values. Nonetheless, I think that new values are emerging, or values that, to a certain extent, already existed, but were well hidden and over-powered by the reality people are facing. It is has become very difficult to find places where that attitude of "I will find the solution myself" is overcome.

It is true that there is a strong presence of competition in the popular neighborhoods. These relations lead to problems of authority and roles: many comrades, including those in the MTD, think that having a position of responsibility in the movement means being "the authority" figure. That is capitalism's logic.

If people get together or meet up, it is generally to pass the time, so that time passes, but not with a sense of solidarity or community. It is to fill time because they don't have anything to do in life.

Sometimes, when someone approaches us about participating in the movement, it is out of an internal interest. We see that the comrade is not showing disinterest, but rather that they have an implicit interest, and that is why they take a step forward.

In moments of crisis, interest arises, but in another form, and labels get attached to things: "I did this and that." This is something else that needs to be overcome and that has to do with how we are built: with the idea that it is not worth doing anything unless we can receive double in return. Then, one thinks about millions of dollars, not about dignified housing with their basic needs met, but rather mansions.

2. Unemployment

What is it like not having work here in the neighborhood? This seems obvious, because this is a movement of "those without work" and, in general, the whole world "knows" what it means to be unemployed as a sociological category. But, what does it mean to be unemployed in terms of lived experience?

When people approach us, they usually expect us to solve the problem of work. The MTD is not about that: it does not solve the problem of unemployment at all. The MTD is a proposal, a project, that takes this issue of work – in this case of unemployment – as its central focus, but it is much broader. It is about building something that has to do with dignity, with the struggle for health, for education. We are not looking to replace the category of the proletariat with that of the unemployed, for example. It is about another type of construction.

For many years, prisons have been filled with people from the neighborhood due to delinquency, drugs. Here we are creating an environment to give young people the chance to not have to go out to steal, although many have relapsed. We have comrades who say quite specifically: "I do not earn enough money to handle issues of severe illnesses." In the movement, they found a space to take back what it means to be responsible for a task, to have an occupation, which gets them away from those groups that can lead to negative consequences, because these kids take one or two pills and go out and do silly things. This is being noticed, although they bring more than a few difficulties to the movement, because they bring their whole life here to the movement. But we decided to respect them, with their life stories, and not marginalize them because they consume drugs and have weapons, and instead develop a relationship of respect with them. At the same time, they are developing a type of respect and esteem among themselves. It builds a positive relationship that they are a part of and recreates common codes that used to exist, even among kids who were involved in theft. One of the consequences of drugs was that the codes broke, but a sort of recovery is created through the feeling that they are not marginalized, but accepted as they are.

This creates a guideline for reconstructing values, codes, and a life in common. There were some neighbors who could not even be in the same room together and now they are participating in the same project, although there is still a lot of work to be done in the neighborhood. We have made a big effort, for example, in the area of cleanliness, in the eradication of junkyards. We have not yet solved the problem of unemployment but we created possibilities for living together. We are not even solving the problem of hunger, there is much to do, but what we are achieving, and this is fundamental to us, is recovering what it means to be human. We always say that one day we will have resources, but the human connection, the relationship between comrades, no one can give you that. And this is what we are trying to achieve. Here unemployment is historic, it has existed for many years, but the saddest thing has been the destruction of values and the ability to live together.

We have been talking about the consequences of this idea – which has become very widespread because of capitalism – of individual salvation and the effect of a very standardized and ideological image of success. But we know that capitalism does not only promise a future salvation, but rather what it primarily shows us is that it is very unlikely that people in these neighborhoods will be able to save themselves. Does this not destroy social bonds? The simple fact that if you are unemployed, you live as someone who is excluded, rejected, do you not resent this? Have young people's expectations, even of saving themselves individually, been destroyed?

This has to do with what you were saying about the comrades who "give up": it is not about the traditional figure who believes that, after a lot of hard effort and work, individual success is waiting for them. What happens to those who give up, and especially, their children?

That is how it is, here capitalism has two faces: on the one hand, the idea that success comes from gaining power, moving up; and on the other hand, behavior which is pathological in my opinion: depression, giving up, or not doing anything, or taking out everything produced by unemployment by abusing their wives, children, or neighbors.

3. Horizontality and struggle

You told us that there are comrades who equate having responsibility in the movement with the right to command other comrades. Since the MTD-S makes a major effort to sustain all its work based on principles of horizontality: How are leadership and its different modes practiced and experienced? What obstacles have you encountered with the forms of protagonism and participation among members of the movement?

What we do is that we constantly revise our agreements. Because we handle everything through agreements: when we go out to block a highway, when we create a working group or in any other area of the movement. Many of our agreements emerged from neighborhood meetings discussing the criteria for building together, and we always come back to those definitions. We have also spent a lot of time analyzing the harm caused by individualist positions. One thing that has helped us is that we always fully discuss the criteria before starting a group and these criteria are always defined by the entire movement. For example, in our productive enterprises, education and training come first, and then you can produce and go out and sell things, training both in terms of production and the political element. That is how we operate: political education is a fundamental tool that ensures that we are able to build together.

We understand capacity-building and political education in broad terms: this project, for example, is an educational activity for us, but so is a roadblock, because we discuss how to carry it out, what happened, what failed. We engage in capacity-building and education every day, and we do so based on the criteria that we have defined. There are requirements that change according to the situation, and there are others that are more general that are the foundation of the movement. For example, we discussed if we wanted a leader or if we would prefer to have a horizontal organization, if we wanted a group to make the decisions or if we wanted to make decisions in an assembly. Direct democracy is one of the unchangeable criteria.

Our movement takes the form of a struggle, and that is what we encourage in order to achieve the things we want. That is another one of our agreements: to participate in the movement, there has to be an agreement that this is a movement of struggle, that we will change things here through fighting for them. But the struggle does not only consist of blockading roads or confronting the police, rather it is an everyday struggle, it is a struggle against our old way of thinking in order to incorporate a new form of thought in which relationships are based on solidarity, the collective, and comrades.

Secondly, each group establishes some of its own criteria that change depending on the specific situation. For example, the question of whether or not we work when it rains. This depends on the group: if it is a group that works outside then generally they don't work, but instead they can watch a movie, discuss, work on capacity-building.

In most projects, there is a group of people who handle the majority of the tasks. Whether because they show more responsibility or are more willing to commit, it ends up creating a delegation of information and of powers to a certain group of comrades, which places them in the center of the organization. This tendency can be seen in many experiences. The group that is placed at the center, even if it is against the will of the movement and of the group in question, then finds itself in difficult position: it is increasingly difficult to effectively collectivize their knowledge and responsibilities. What mechanisms have you found for avoiding or reversing this tendency of delegation?

There is always a level of dependency, especially when comrades are new to the movement, because they look for the person in the group who has the most experience, or simply the person who can speak the best or who can carry out the task the best. It creates a dependency that we say is ok, but only during a certain stage, not forever. The way of reversing this situation is to socialize knowledges, and to do so, we work with popular education. We create spaces where all the comrades can develop their talents, their abilities, their contributions, in an infinite number of responsibilities. There are comrades who have trade union experience, others who are more uninhibited, and others who are terrified of taking on responsibility. So, we have to work constantly so that no one is left doing nothing. That is where overcoming the figure of the leader comes in. Additionally, delegation has to be rotating; it has to be for a limited time, determined by the comrades, depending on the needs of the situation.

One year ago, there was a great deal of growth in the movement and there is still a great deal of dependency. But we always said that those who have a supporting role, are there to create bonds, to accompany, but never to decide. They provide accompaniment, but never a solution, they are not the ones who decide what must be done. We know that this is going to take time, but there are very encouraging signs, because people who used to be quiet, who avoided participating, not only come to complete their four hours of community work, but they have also started to work on other tasks and activities. This is inspiring, but we can't speed up the time frames. There are leaderships that are positive because they don't exclude anyone, because they help others to grow. But there are also leaderships that hoard, that do not create participation, that impose authoritarianism. This requires constant revision in the democracy of the movement, in life as such, to prepare for other challenges. Because life is not pure, we can't say that we have one hundred percent participation, direct democracy and horizontality, but we know that this is the right path.

Another important thing is making sure that when a comrade used to be a leader and is now stepping out of that position, that their life and commitment doesn't stop. It is complicated, because these are often mechanisms of compensation and everyone wants to be loved; we all have our egos. So, we try to be in a situation of helping and illuminating, but without burning ourselves. It is one thing to help, to illuminate, to be available, and something else to not allow the other to grow.

The movement is not merely an ideological political organization, that is, a group that is validated by its "proposals" and "opinions" about "this or that" (although of course those proposals and opinions do exist). The MTD-S has a form of intervention that we think is very powerful. It is the capacity to directly target sociability, values, and the ways in which people resolve all of life's problems. Honestly, we have always thought that concrete counter-power is not a political force, but rather but a potencia for the production of values, ways of existence, that are superior to those that capitalism produces in situation.

Along this line, we would like to ask you to talk about how you work in relation to the deepest cores of sociability and intimacy in the neighborhood. In fact, if the movement were not to question prior modes of sociability, it would simply be a structure that would reproduce dominant values.

Is it possible to recreate a society around alternative values without, at the same time working on the level of the roles that are imposed by the family, belief systems, education, etc.? Is this community organization, this collective experience, modifying the family structure?

Yes, in the little time that we have been organizing things have been changing. In fact, there was very little participation in the neighborhood assembly at first. It is normal, not only in the MTD, but in other organizations as well, among parents in relation to school and even at church, for there to be less involvement in these neighborhoods. We are happy to see that in our experience this pattern is being broken. We see comrades who not only come to an assembly, but also go to marches or roadblocks, which are things that, until recently, provoked a great deal of fear, a lot of resistance. There are spaces that are being created, and people are starting to feel that they are necessary: to be a part of something bigger than their family. Relationships are generated that continue and show a growth in comrades for whom their families are no longer enough. This is evident when many people stay behind to talk even after the assembly has ended. Some comrades say that they only started to truly live when they came here. It is a very intense experience to find life's meaning in communal spaces, where relations are created and values are being revived. Some comrades say that they would keep coming even if the benefit packages stopped. What motivates them is the possibility of generating relations of friendship, of camaraderie, of community. For many, the MTD is their family.

4. A little bit of history

Can you tell us about the movement's history? How did the expulsion from the Church happen? Is it connected to the issue of how authority and capitalism work in the neighborhood?

Yes, I think that it has to do with a way of understanding participation, using a conceptualization that is now in crisis. There was an important experience of *comunidades eclesiales de base* [community-based churches] in this neighborhood, based on community participation and supporting people. The higher-ups put a stop to that process for a reason. In 1987, the Church took on a new orientation in which liberation theology and community-based churches –expressions of liberation theology – started being cut off. They were replaced by traditional priests, which created commotion and crisis.

When we arrived in Solano with the other priest, Antonio, we had an idea of communities as an expression of participation, of connecting to the problems latent in the neighborhood, so we started recuperating what they had tried to shut down. At the same time, an environment was generated that caused a lot of conflict because there were other sectors that had another dynamic, another vision of power. That is, they understood being on a council, being part of the church, as power that only belonged to a few and that others must be subordinated to this authority. We were attempting to democratize, so we tried to focus on the most urgent issue: unemployment. We started to have assemblies of the unemployed inside church buildings. But this dynamic ran counter to decisions that the diocese leadership had already taken, since it put their relationship with the government at risk. Therefore, the bishop asked me to get the unemployed people out of the church, and we responded that it is the people who have to decide. The Bishop said no, that I was the problem: "what community, what assembly? You're responsible for this!" That was the discussion, and he ended up treating us as rebels, agitators, usurpers. The Church plays a very important role in accompanying capitalism, because it produces hierarchical relationships.

There is the figure of the priest who, while being very progressive, ends up favoring social trends that do not exactly go in the direction of popular organizations. Nonetheless, there are other experiences in which the priest appears as a sort of authority that people appeal to when building community. I am not only taking about Solano, but the hundreds of places in Latin America were the priest is called up for a type of knowledge and authority that is not necessarily an oppressive hierarchy, but can also be a reference point where there is nothing else, where everything has been destroyed.

Yes, the key element is that in this area we managed to demystify, to a large degree, the figure of the priest as the maximum authority and a representative of God on Earth. Here the priest was more a coordinator, someone who facilitated the work of articulation, of conflict resolution. There are more conservative sectors, even in Solano that questioned the rest of the people: "How can it be that an ordinary person has more control than the priest?" they would say. There are people who think that the priest's word is absolute and the same goes for the bishops.

Definitely there are many places in Latin America where priests have played a role in supporting community experiences. The Landless Workers' Movement (MST) in Brazil is one example. That is, there are bishops who are coherent, who are progressive not only in their discourse, but also in practice.

5. Grassroots organization

When we published the Borradores de Investigación [Research Drafts][12] *regarding "the piqueterx struggle" we received a great deal of criticism, especially from people affiliated with the Argentine Central Workers' Union (CTA). We were basically reproached for having such an acute criticism of Luis D'Elía's movement and for idealizing the experience of Solano too much. We then were obliged – by our critical friends – to improve the quality of our pamphlet and to go into more depth about the problems that were emerging in regards to representation, the temptation of the political, and all these sorts of problems – that are surely similar to many other movements – and that we pointed to in the Drafts.*

We thought that what would be interesting, then, would be to show to what extent the differences between these experiences can be found at the level of how decisions are made when confronting these common problems, rather than hiding the fact that these alternative modes face exactly the same obstacles.

To start then: How is the MTD Solano organized? How do you organize so that the movement is not considered as that which has all the answers and solves all the problems? How do you operate so that the movement does not constitute itself as a power that impedes the circulation of new knowledges and forms of protagonism?

Here in Solano the movement emerged in response to a concrete need in the neighborhood, in relation to which we started to come together. I think that there was no recipe to start with, but rather we are making it up as we go along, and, as we continue organizing, new things start coming up.

The assembly is the most important body, it is where proposals are debated, where the main decisions are made: the plans for struggle, the creation of new areas, the election of delegates from each neighborhood.

In the neighborhoods, on the other hand, there are working groups, composed of ten or twenty people that choose two or three delegates; there is no precise number, but always more than one.

In each work area, these elected comrades form a commission, a place for evaluating and discussing any difficulties that arise. The group is not there to resolve problems because resolutions are made in the assembly. When work arises in new neighborhoods, each group elects two delegates to join a general commission, whose

---

12   We are referring to a report that we prepared in August of 2001, after the emergence of the National Piquetero Movement. The report aimed to show that very different forms of thinking and acting were hidden within the social phenomena called the *piqueterx*. That draft was based on work done with the MTD-S.

main function is the articulation between neighborhoods.

Lastly, there are areas that have emerged from necessity. The press group, for example, arose when we started having a relationship with the media and because we started making denunciations; the production group that has to do with planning; the economic area, that handles the movement's budget; capacity-building and popular education; security, which was created for the roadblocks; administration, that is responsible for everything that has to do with the unemployment benefits and jobs plans, the development of projects, and the relationship with the ministry; merchandise, which is not operational right now because we have not received groceries in a long time; the land; and the area of institutional relations, that operates when, as a result of the roadblocks, we have to go to a meeting with the ministry.

Assemblies are often spaces where people express pre-established positions, as if it were a plebiscite in which people do not actively participate other than choosing between already decided options; of better yet, they legitimate positions that had already been defined. We know that it is not easy to create an assembly that becomes a true space of collective thought.

Participation fundamentally depends on the process of growth in each neighborhood. There are places where there is a lot of debate, and usually, there is a lot of agreement on fundamental ideas, because there has been more time for collective work. In the smaller and newer neighborhoods, we use certain questions and exercises to encourage participation.

I think that it is very important to continually return to the criteria and principles that have already been discussed at length, because they constitute the pillars of the movement and often frame the discussions. For example, this is a movement in which it is very clear that there are no ambitions of power, and therefore, the possibility of running for office is eliminated. This does not mean that there are not moments when problems and positions arise that question the organization's criteria.

That is why I think it has to do with maturity. It is a process and we cannot say that the assemblies are truly democratic. There are often debates that last for hours. There are times when we have to settle things with a vote, but generally we seek consensus. There have been tensions; there have been many crises, in different neighborhoods, and with the delegates. The last action plans left a hole on the road and that had repercussions. But we have not suffered divisions, which shows that there is a collective exercise that allows us to grow and keep moving forward.

With respect to coordination and the political connections that are established with different groups, perhaps it is more difficult to sustain this dynamic, because you enter into relations with groups that do not have the same practices (beyond what they say about themselves or what, in their heads, they want to happen).

Recently you were telling us how you resolve problems inside the neighborhood, how you make decisions. There is a criterion of responsibility used that sustains the experience. This horizontality of responsibilities creates the conditions for a common, sovereign experience of thinking, and at the same time, of practice. But how can these modes of recreating existential agreements be expanded; how can you recreate these original projects when you are working at the level of coordination between different organizations?

There is a great deal of respect, and also, we handle things based on the agreements that we make. But within the MTD coordinator, there are groups that have another form of construction, other characteristics.

It is more complicated when we go to other spaces, in which there are other movements or organizations besides those of the unemployed.

There is a way of thinking about organization, that is very widespread among popular movements, that prioritizes institutional terms. The question that are made there are: How do we make a diagram that is democratic? How do we create a formula that guarantees internal democracy? Often, these end up being empty spaces where nothing happens.

It seems to me that this simulation of democracy tends to exist in organizations that see base building as a means to other ends.

Yes, and this could have to do with a form of militant activity that is based on trying to maintain a "model" (a set of knowledges) of how to constitute the movement. This especially includes comrades who, without bad intentions, end up with an ideological "model" that is completely external to the situation in which they work, and they appear, all of a sudden, with criteria that are totally dogmatic about how things should be, placing external criteria above the collective experience.

This militant "shortcut" saves times at the beginning of the work: the road of creating, of thinking collectively.

Therefore, when you talk about the organizational criteria that you work with, one cannot help but be a little distrusting, due to having heard these criteria in other places where they "acted as if they practiced" those criteria, but in reality, the areas of thought were controlled by "political astuteness" and those "militant knowledges." I think there is something in how you all think about construction that goes beyond what you are telling us about your form of organizing.

In some neighborhoods, we are destroying the image of the delegate, because we had a major crisis due to authoritarian and selfish attitudes. We said that we don't want to repeat this model any more, that nobody should be able to bring us down, and that we had to work in a more participatory way. What we did was to put everything on rotating bases. We made a timeline for the general commission. Ultimately, we didn't want any more delegates, so we all participated. What remains to be seen is how to make sure that the function that delegates served, which was communicating with other neighborhoods, articulating tasks, etc. is still guaranteed.

What was destroyed was the role of the delegate, not its function.

Yes, the role of the delegate as an authority. If this role was taken on as a form of power, it needs to be destroyed.

It is interesting to us that when you speak of a comrade who acted badly, who made a mistake, you talk about them as someone who has not received enough training or education. Why is that?

The problem with these comrades is that when a crisis appears, instead of resolving it, they complicate it more with personal issues. Instead of thinking of a more political response, they fall back on the personal.

Then, it is something that has to do with the collective, not that they lack the capacity to think. We are referring to the issue of putting personal interests about the collective. Furthermore, for us, it is not only that individual comrade's responsibility, but rather a collective responsibility, that belongs to all of us as a whole.

You said that it was in this neighborhood where the organization first emerged. How did it emerge in the others?

In all the neighborhoods it emerged from peoples' requests. Some, such as those of La Florida and Monteverde approached us here. Others – for example IAPI, La Sarita, Avellaneda – emerged from the roadblocks. We were blocking roads in that area, and neighborhoods residents approached us and got hooked on the roadblocks. But they all emerged from a proposal from the neighborhood, we never went out to offer anything. Even here in San Martín, the movement emerged from a proposal from comrades who had problems of unemployment. It's not like we said: "let's create a Movement of the Unemployed."

The comrades from other neighborhoods asked us to visit and tell them about what we were doing. Then there would be a conversation about whether they wanted to organize themselves like or us if they wanted to do something different. It was never an imposition. That is how the experience began. There were no problems in other neighborhoods for not wanting to integrate themselves into our requirements. Yes, some things were debated again, along the way, such as the marches, but not in terms of doing away with more important criteria.

6. Roadblocks

I think that the roadblocks made apathy explode, but in a different way. We woke the country up from the sweet dreams that Menem was selling and that whole type of politics, and we were like the eruption of another light. Along with other struggles we made the country wake up from the sweet dreams of postmodernity. *Piqueterxs* was the name that they gave us, and it was our way of speaking to society as a whole, of telling them that there were other forms of struggle, to show our fire, as well as our dignity.

How did this idea come about? How were the roadblocks organized here?

The roadblocks emerged in the interior, in Cutral Có, Tartagal, Mosconi, and Santiago del Estero and spread across the whole country, cutting off the circulation of free trade that feeds the metropolis. At that time, people started taking up the roadblocks as a form of struggle here in Buenos Aires, but there was tremendous debate over whether accepting the *Trabajar* benefits packages was the correct form of action or not. Some said that this was creating a welfarism or clientelism. Instead of getting involved in that debate, what we did was to put it into practice. At that time, we were organized in the parish and the question of struggle started to be raised. Taking over the municipal offices was something that was always discussed, until the first roadblock took place. The first one was more or less improvised and some comrades were arrested. Little by little it became clear that a new form of struggle was emerging.

But the most important thing is that we started to grow; we started creating productive project projects, engaging in capacity-building, popular education, and all those things are more important than being out on the street. Because being on the street is what is seen, and it seems like everything is out there, but the struggle is fundamentally everything we were doing before. In reality, if we went out on the streets it is because we were already organized.

But the media insists on talking about the unemployed who go out with their faces covered, totally marginalized beings, worthless beings who have never worked.

It is good to clarify that at the beginning all the left and progressives accused us of asking for charity, being reformists, of begging at the feet of the master, and they did not recognize the organization's main slogan: work, dignity, and social change. It was obvious that it was not only about the benefits packages, although it did lead to the death of many organizations for whom it was only about getting the benefits and going home.

On the other hand, the roadblocks have changed a great deal. We went to our first roadblock with our faces uncovered, we had some rocks that we had half hidden so that no one would be scared. It was a process, we suffered different types of repression, and we started to cover our faces so that the state couldn't identify us. We also started to use violence as self-defense: not throwing sticks or stones to attack, but rather to defend ourselves. But also, it's important to emphasize that the roadblocks and the benefits packages are but one element of the struggle; they are not the fundamental elements.

The benefits programs are the reality that we can organize around. That is, we don't have the opportunity to take over a factory. What we don't share at all with other organizations is using neighborhood organizations, and the real work that they do, as an "excuse" for other ends.

There were difficult moments in the first roadblocks. But something changed after Mosconi.[13] Following those events, we saw changes in comrades' consciousnesses. Before they insisted that nothing was going happen, we had to make an effort so that comrades would not be scared, and most of the time we would hide our sticks and slingshots. We had intense debates about whether or not we should cover our faces. Through this process, we started to understand that it was necessary to have a certain level of self-defense: we could not go out on the street as easy targets for the police and the comrades in charge of security could not allow the military to see their faces. In the roadblocks that we did with congress of La Matanza, the CTA insisted that we take off our masks. We took the issue to an assembly and decided that if they were going to take away our masks, we were going to leave. The system

---

13   This is in reference to the 2001 uprising in General Mosconi, in the province of Salta, in response to layoffs following the privatization of the oil industry. The heavy suppression of the uprising left two people dead.

considers roadblocks to be a crime, but we believe they are legitimate. This is a fundamental change that we went through as an organization.

We know that the fact that your organization organizes workshops, projects, capacity-building, that you have a constant collective life, sets you apart from other organizations of the unemployed. How are these differences manifested when it comes to organizing roadblocks?

I have experience in other roadblocks and I have seen the difference in regards to the organization, the security requirements, the discipline of the comrades. In our roadblocks, it shocks others to see that if a comrade notices someone drinking, they request that the person leave due to security reasons. This is an ongoing process in the neighborhoods, in comrades' lives, because we are talking about comrades who, only a year ago, would vote for thirty pesos, or would go out to steal so that they could survive.

What sustains and solidifies this transformation is political education. We do not impose a requirement that comrades do not drink, but rather this is discussed in the assemblies. And, fundamentally, it is not the coordinators who say that people should not drink, rather we search for a consensus, we discuss why it is not worth it. This is the big difference, not whether or not we cover our faces, or who has the bigger stick.

When did you all get the first benefit packages that you started to organize for?

In 1997, after our first marches to the municipal offices, we received 50 benefits packages. We did not block the roads; we marched to the Secretary of Employment of the municipality. The first benefit packages we therefore received from the municipality. We won the autonomy to manage the plans after two roadblocks.

Was there a conscious decision to change that relationship with the state at some moment?

Yes, and that is what differentiated us from other organizations; today many organizations are proposing this. The problem basically was that the municipality pressured comrades to stop organizing. Of the 120 comrades who started the work, today only five or six remain in the MTD. We realized that it did not make sense to do something that would benefit the system which we were trying to overturn.

We have spoken several times of the heterogeneity that exists in the piqueterx movement, how would you explain this?

The differences that are being noted with other organizations primarily emerged because many still work in a very traditional way: "we will take power from above and change things from there." And we say: from below, without proposing to take power, we will engage in our struggle. We are below and we do not want to leave there, we want to stay below; we will always be rebels.

We are below and we do not want to rise. Here there are comrades who stand out, but what you will not find are aspirations to be leaders. Guiding the movement is a constant process that takes place among all of us.

In any case, these differences don't allow us to lose sight of the fact that it is important to articulate, that it is important to coordinate, that it is necessary to continue to debate and make agreements, struggling together. We do not say that we have the truth and others don't. We see that there are differences in movement building, but all these differences can be coordinated, as long as issues of social change and dignity are being raised, and not using the people to win elections, for example.

I heard some piqueterx comrades saying that in their daily lives they used to feel like they were "shit," "the forgotten," "left behind," and that in the roadblocks they feel different, that they "have power," that "decisions are made there."

That is true, it is a space of freedom, an autonomous zone, and it is the only place where the military and police do not treat you like trash. In the roadblocks, the military speaks to you like: "excuse me, we came to negotiate." If those same police saw you alone on the street, they would beat the shit out of you.

It is true that we control an area in the roadblocks, but I think that the comrades feel that they are recuperating this power through the organization, not only in the roadblocks, but it is the organization that creates strength. For example, today the comrades that are doing the work of putting up street signs, they put up signs that say "MTD" and an arrow showing where our building is. These are strong signs of counter-power.

You said that there were comrades who had a more instrumental relationship with the movement, and that they only come to receive their benefits, how is this reflected in the roadblocks?

The majority of comrades who have approached the movement recently, more than eighty per cent, came exclusively out of a concrete necessity. They need something to eat, they don't have food, they don't have a job, they don't have anything. But, when there is a process, things change, adrenaline starts flowing and they start feeling the need to organize themselves.

You said that when you take to the streets, you are saying "no" to the model, "no" to a system. I think that this can be understood in two ways: on the one hand, that the model failed and that you all represent the moment in which the victims make themselves present, in a sort of Christian sense, in which the people never escape this place of victimization that attests to misery: those who "are stuck outside," who beg, shamelessly, so that they are not forgotten. But there is another way of seeing this issue, in which the model did not fail and exclusion does not exist, because there is no place to be included and that is what the exploited are: desirable variables of the system. Thus, we feel like the position of the majority of those participating in the roadblocks is not that of the victim, but that there is a very clear subjective will to actively think and work.

We don't want inclusion. I don't want to be exploited again. I don't want to have Fortabat or the Macris as my boss again, that's for sure. I'm not fighting for them to go back to exploiting me. Personally, I feel, and many other comrades do as well, that we are not here for inclusion; that what we are doing is something else. One thing that we are certain about is precisely what we don't want as an organization. The novelty of each day lies in discovering where it is we want to go and what it is that we are building. This is not something that is closed; it is not finished or predetermined, rather, we are continuously reflecting. The organization is dynamic; it changes and we reflect on this. It is true that you can notice the adrenaline when we go out to block a road, but the novel element of the movement is that this is not separated from our everyday lives. That is the reality of the organization: what is expressed in the roadblock has to be constructed in our everyday lives because it won't work any other way. We don't find an answer to this in the system, so we have to make another history. When we make demands, they are not about inclusion, we only request what helps us be able to continue organizing ourselves.

How do you decide to carry out a roadblock, who decides how and where?

Each area informs the others about what is happening. Then, according to that information, an action plan is proposed in each neighborhood. There is a discussion about whether to have a march or a roadblock. First, the decision is made in all the neighborhood assemblies, later, in the commission, consensus is reached building on what was expressed in the neighborhoods. Based on the proposals, we can see our capacity. For reasons of security, in the assemblies we never say where the roadblock will take place. The method is decided there, but not the details.

The roles and groups are decided in the assemblies. For example, in the assembly we decide who will do first aid, kitchen duties, security. In other words, the groups coordinate the activities and there is someone with the role of connecting the different areas, who is also elected on a rotating basis.

It seems as though security and the political criteria of the roadblock are always responses to the organization's internal considerations and not to the needs of the political conjuncture, or to eventual external support.

Yes, but these internal necessities are much more than our "economic needs." For example, when we blocked a road because of what happened in Mosconi, it had to do with our identity. Because if they harmed someone in Mosconi, it also has to do with us, even though it does not directly affect us in Solano.

Or when we blocked Pueyrredón Bridge because of risks of repression in La Matanza, and we said to the government: "If you are repressing them over there, you will also have to repress us over here." We saw that they were beating our brothers and sisters (despite D'Elia and Alderete) and we had to go out and fight for them. But, yes, we do not build for the conjuncture. We are not interested in electoral politics, whether we vote tomorrow or not.

Another example is when Patricia Bullrich organized an offensive. We said: "we have to go out and protest because they wanted to break us as an organization." The problem there was that it was impeding us from continuing with our work. What we never do is go out to protest when one of the powers of the superstructure is calling for it, because they have a predetermined political analysis of why it must be done. Instead, we analyze the situations ourselves.

We don't dispute the space with anyone, nor do we want to be anyone's vanguard. We are building and articulating our thoughts with others who are transforming their own situations. We are not interested in going to La Matanza to agitate and win space there. That is not how we conceive of political action. Yes, we think that grassroots organizing must continue, but it is the comrades from La Matanza who have to fight for this. We seek to coordinate with those who are building movements, but we don't dispute any type of space.

Nor are we blindly committed to the grassroots, as some accuse us. We have a political project and, in fact, we know how to analyze the conjuncture, but we do it in the neighborhoods and with the people. Therefore, our analysis is even more complete; they cannot say that we don't have a strategy and that we need a political structure to direct us. That is a lie. The movement is a political tool in itself, everyone, all the members of the movement, shape that tool and they all carry out that analysis. When they ask us what our political project is, we say: it is politicization from below, but completely. It is a comprehensive formation of the person in every way. Everything counts and is important.

We do not think that we need to form a front that traverses the entire nation in order to achieve something. I don't think that there will be a single alliance or a front that will take power, there will be many fronts.

7. Autonomy from the state

What is your relationship with the state in regards to the benefits packages?

It changes a lot because, depending on the moment, the state applies some kind or pressure or another. They are always more generous during elections. They use this playbook and so do we. Therefore, we say: "this is all nice because it is convenient for them, so let us take what we can, let's take advantage of the situation." That is the permanent relation, changing according to the conjuncture.

Nonetheless, we always keep a distance. Although we think that at certain moments it would be worth getting closer to the provincial government because they are doing some good things. But this does not mean that we are married to them. It depends on our tactics. We are not going to go out and target everyone, because we are the most revolutionary, that is not our politics. But nor are we conciliators or negotiators. We are neither one nor the other. We just know how to calculate the situation, who we need to target and we do so at the appropriate moment.

What is clear is that today we depend on what we take from the state in order to organize ourselves.

Do you feel like the state has the capacity to destroy this form of relationship that you have imposed on it?

I think that they have the capacity to take away all of our subsidies and benefits packages. But what they don't know is that we have consolidated something that goes beyond the material element. I am sure that, beyond the benefits, many of us would keep participating in the organization. They can take away the subsidies, send the repressive apparatus, and everything they want, but what we have here is a different way of thinking, and that is something they will not be able to destroy.

We tighten our waists against the state in order to sustain ourselves and endure what we can. We are not going to risk everything against the state. We are building something different from the repressive state, from below. I always say that the world is round and they are always trying to corner us, but they can't; they want to put us in a corner, but we always find a way to keep moving.

8. The conjuncture

There is one question that keeps coming back to us, and, of course, to which we don't have answers. Do you feel like you are a movement in the middle of a decisive field of political struggles? Do you feel like you are in a violent struggle for power, consensus, state recognition, and positive media coverage? Do you think this is how the experience is organized for the state? Or rather, do you think that they see you as a group that is occasionally bothersome and that they give you the minimum necessary to pacify you?

It's complicated. I think that the eviction from the church, at the beginning, was a serious attempt to cut off the roots of the organization that was emerging. At that time, it was very difficult to win any concessions. It was not like you would go out and protest and they would throw a bunch of subsidies at you to keep you calm. Here in Solano, some comrades have suffered harassment and persecutions; they burned down the house of one comrade, and have threatened others. In other words, on the one hand, they give you something, but on the other they pressure you with the *punteros*.[14] I think that the government started taking us seriously when we started growing and starting coordinating with other groups. Because our strength lies in unity for the struggle and for legitimacy.

We know that we will have complete autonomy when we are able to sustain all the projects and things that we are doing without needing the state to provide subsidies for any of it. But today the situation is such that we need those resources that allow us to develop the organization. On the other hand, we know that in December they are going to make cuts to those subsidies, they are going to implement major austerity measures. While we, as Solano or as the coordinator, will be able to do it one day, today we cannot stop it alone. But our idea is to make sure

---

14   Local political brokers, who work as intermediaries between political parties and the poor, often wield their access to resources and financial power and, if that doesn't work, violence, as a way to ensure allegiance. – Trans.

that they do not screw us over; in other words, in this sense it is a defensive struggle.

Yes, we are not interested in continuing confrontation for the sake of confrontation. I think that they know that. We are interested in having the resources to be able to consolidate ourselves. Because the objective is not that De La Rua falls tomorrow, but rather the issue of autonomy.

We are not motivated by whether this or that government takes power or sabotaging the other. Nor are we fighting so that Ruckauf does not become president, or something like that, because our problems are not resolved by whether or not he becomes president. And nor do we think that we are the force that can stop Ruckauf from becoming president. Now, if those guys do stupid things and to not fulfill their promises, we will be there. And we will be there no matter who the president is.

Our action plans always emerge from an analysis of our situation, and they are always defensive, until this dependence on the state becomes less necessary.

9. New forms of militant commitment

Tell us about the MTD-Solano's militancy? How is commitment understood in experiences that no longer seek to take power?

It is difficult because the movement is constantly being redefined. In any case, we do not respond to any traditional forms of commitment. We have comrades who, up until two years ago, were political *punteros*, and today are militants of the MTD, and they don't even know where Che Guevara was born. Or other comrades who don't have any previous activist experience and they started becoming activists when they joined the MTD, and, in a way, they are the ones who, through their commitment, make it possible for us to move forward.

The issue of not seeking state power is very important when we speak of the type of commitment that is produced here in Solano. Power is built in the answers that we are finding for what we are looking for as free men and women. That is where commitment is defined, in the day to day construction that takes place from below.

But what does it mean to be a militant of the MTD, what are the requirements for someone to be considered an MTD militant?

The issue is that we almost never speak of militants; we speak of committed comrades, of comrades who take on responsibilities to different degrees. There are comrades who work in the area of capacity-building and education, and nothing else. Perhaps in other organizations, the militant is someone who puts in twenty-four hours a day and leaves behind their own life. We highly value comrades who do capacity-building work, or who are in charge of an area and carry out their duty, or someone who is just starting to commit themselves, and each one is as valid as the others. We do not speak of militants, we speak of committed comrades.

Because, on the other hand, what moral authority do we have to say whether or not someone is a militant or a great organizer? I think that the only way of classifying someone is through their commitment, for being there, wagering on the movement. So, we speak of degrees of commitment.

But it is not that those degrees of commitment are considered in terms of a hierarchy. A comrade can leave behind their whole life, but it will not be to occupy a leadership role. Other organizations work with cadres and we have materials that explain how to organize these traditional organizations. At first I thought that is how we would have to organize, because I thought that it would be the way to get more comrades to commit so that we would not be left with only a few of us sustaining the movement. But I finally realized that comrades take on more responsibility, and real responsibility, when they participate in the work, when they commit themselves to the dynamic of the movement.

We are always insisting on trying to generate spaces, all the spaces necessary, for the comprehensive education and training of all the comrades. It is not about "training cadres," but rather of comrades who want to understand the movement. But it is not that we are all equal and that we do not progress, that we are all round or square. We try to create spaces, like the project that we are doing with you all, or the history projects. And some people participate in these and some do not, or some come every once and a while, and others ask "how did that go?"

Here we don't think, as society wants us to, of comrades as being part of the market and being valued for their market value, for their economic benefit. Here there is another form of struggle, something different; we are trying to recuperate values of rebelliousness and dignity, of honesty, creativity, and beauty. We organize based on those values and comrades who approach our organization do so for those reasons. Therefore, we fundamentally work with the slogan, "work, dignity, and social change." In terms of social change, we are interested in rebelliousness. It is through that collective search that comrades become committed.

We have discussed the differences between the MTD, and for example, the movement of the unemployed in Mosconi, which is more spontaneous and less structured.

It is because the social reality is not the same. Here in Buenos Aires social bonds are very weak: if you are unemployed and you go out to a roadblock, your neighbor who has to go to work will run you over with their car. Here people are more fucked, more burnt out, and there is total individualism. Here is where capitalism has destroyed the most, where we suffered a great ideological defeat. This is most apparent is in the large urban centers, in the capital cities, where there is the most consumerism, selfishness, technological advancement, and all the promises of capitalism. It is not like that in Mosconi, where the community is more integrated and share the same fate.

And what are the challenges the MTD faces in regards to these differences?

We face a much greater challenge because we don't simply have an external enemy, but we also have an internal enemy. That is where the problem lies: the individual who approaches our movement usually does not come with a life project, they come because of a concrete need, and they bring all their vices with them. The level of human putrefaction is much greater here than in Mosconi. Here, for a long time, capitalism managed to cancel out the meaning of words such as solidarity, camaraderie, commitment. On the other hand, in Mosconi, they are only fighting for work, and therefore they use other methods of organizing. Here we are mostly focused on issues of dignity and social change. For example, we are trying to work on the idea of an alternative economy.

You all are elaborating a very large project. From what we see, it is not about calling attention to a set of sporadic demands, but rather something more profound. It gives us the sensation that you all are immersed in a process of practical thought and self-affirmation, in a becoming that is real. While many other social organizations organize around "demands," you work based on active thinking and your strength, that is to say, from a subjective position that is different from that of someone who only has demands.

We try to create practical projects that are not small and medium-sized businesses, but that have other characteristics, that transform labour relations, where it is not the products that are essential, or exchanging labor power for money, but a more expansive project.

It has to do with different realities. The province of Buenos Aires is not the same as the capital city. There you can go out and collect cans to recycle and earn five or six pesos a day; here you won't find a single can. And it is different in the interior of the country; there is another type of poverty there. But it also has to do with the types of political projects. That is also different. Here the issue is that a group of comrades from the MTD started to propose a different way of relating to capitalism, and something different has been generated. We are concerned with how to organize in order to build something else, and guarantee autonomy and encounter.

In reality, the economic poverty is the same. What is more ingrained here is moral and ideological misery.

10. Identity as a search

One could assume that one movement of unemployed workers is not that different from another group of the unemployed because their identity would immediately come from the fact of all being unemployed. That is how, at least some, sociological discourses act, in which an unemployed person is "someone looking for work." And the unemployed would find their identity in that common property: lack. But if, as you all were saying, it is about "fighting to never go back to being an exploited worker," "to change labor relations," then things change radically. The problem of identity is much more complex. There are many ways of understanding what it means to be unemployed.

What we are doing in the movement is a huge battle against the hegemonic fury of globalization that wants to take over cultural values, and thus take over the world. Faced with this globalization, we ask ourselves: What would be the real values of a different civilization? And, to the contrary, what is it that a globalized society values? We know the answer to this: the market, market value, and the person as a commodity to be bought and sold. We try to recuperate and create other cultural and ethical values, with knowledge and creativity.

I think that is it one thing to ask for work, even genuine work, and another thing entirely to demand work and dignity. I am not saying that it is not dignified; for example, to ask Repsol for work or better wages. But what is undignified is exploitation. And I think it is time to start generating other relations. We do not have a finished idea of the forms of production that we want to create, but what we are certain about is that we don't want to generate relations of exploitation. And this is a permanent struggle.

One big debate that we have had is whether to sell food to the market or if should be used to meet comrades' needs. These debates take place within the movement, the debate hasn't ended. That is where identity is constantly being shaped. What we are very clear about is that we want to abolish exploitation; but exploitation is not canceled by having an idea, but rather through a process, little by little.

I will never forget what one comrade once said when we were working on the topic of identity in a popular education workshop. She said: "Here I have gone back to being myself with respect to my work. Because now I am a worker, even if I don't even have a subsidy: I am a worker and I am not exploited."

That is why the apparent contradiction of speaking of unemployed workers is false. Because it would seem that someone who is unemployed cannot be a worker precisely because they lack employment: but we speak of work in another way – one that is more profound – and not only of the laborer.

The condition of being a worker does not come from being exploited, but rather it has to do with an attitude towards life. We try to create spaces where the conversation is not about how to generate exploitation, in other words, not about generating profit.

So, the MTD is not only a movement of the unemployed, rather it is for anyone who wants to work here, under these conditions.

Yes, it is for anyone who wants to recuperate those values that we were talking about before. Because first you have to value yourself as a person, and that is how you feel like a worker: like a human being who has recovered part of their identity. They are workers because they are bringing something to the collective, to the community, and not because they generate market value. If you think that a worker is someone who generates profit, then the unemployed is a pariah in life. But here we are motivated by other values, that are different from those given to us by society.

We said before that more than "training" a "militant-type," what you look for here is commitment. In more specific terms, how do you understand commitment? I ask you because it has caught our attention that other movements of the unemployed quantify militant work going so far as to use a point system, giving comrades points for their participation, and those with most points are the first to receive state benefits. How does it work here?

Here there is no point system. There are collective criteria for organizing: for example, there is an agreement that anything the movement gets is for everyone, for all those who are involved in the struggle. We try not to generate a reliance on state assistance or a paternalistic relation with the state based on welfare; we do not want to form a commission that distributes goods while people stay at home. No, here we want to generate a consciousness of struggle, if you aren't involved in the struggle, you don't get anything.

For example, I see that comrades take on more and more responsibility when they see the need to educate or train themselves, or when they start to participate in capacity-building activities, or when a comrade seriously commits themselves to a productive project, or also when someone brings sandwiches to the roadblock, not only for himself, but for everyone, just because he had some money. There are many different forms of commitment that cannot be measured in words because they are everyday values.

This comrade, for example, joined the movement four months ago, and it was because his wife told him to come to a roadblock. He very quickly started participating in the area of security, and he immediately wanted to take up responsibilities in this area. He did some stupid things, obviously, but the most important thing was that he participated and was committed. All of a sudden, he was spending all his time doing movement things. Now we have to tell him to spend some time at home, because he is here all day. Nobody ever said to him: "You have to be in the organization for a certain amount time, you must meet certain requirements." No, this is a comrade who is always there when you need something. If the comrade is serious, reliable, then, onward! Mistakes are corrected along the way.

There are other comrades who have been here for four years and they still only participate in the projects, the assembly, the roadblocks. But you never see them in the general meetings, in the in specific areas, in the training activities. Nonetheless, they are still committed comrades, only in another way, but still very reliable. We can't even really speak of degrees, better yet of different types of commitment.

11. Resisting virtualization

Turning to the problem of representation: how do you decide who speaks to the media, for example, when you have a roadblock?

What we do is explain the central themes beforehand, the message that we want to transmit, so that anyone can manage.

We try to make it so that it is not always the same person who is speaking to the media or negotiating with the ministry, so that many comrades learn how to do these things, but also so that nobody stands out or could be identified.

Generally, the people in the media look for Alberto and he tells them that there are other comrades who they can talk to. What often happens though is that they make the report and then they come back and interview him. That is because the figure of a priest is very appealing. The problem is that in this way they quickly put labels on people.

What do you mean?

That there is always a leader, that there is always a representative. But neither in the ministry, nor in the media do we have a leader. We are a horizontal and democratic organization and this must also be expressed in those interactions. It is not only expressed in words or on paper, but in concrete practices.

The problem is that *piqueterxs* have become somewhat of a fad recently. You are turned into a star, they see you masked up, and the media is all over you.

But, what risks are associated with the media?

The tricky questions with double meanings. Questions, for example, which speak of violence: why are you masked, why do you have a stick, or a rock, what are you going to do if law enforcement intervenes.

The other day we were blocking Pueyrredón Bridge and there was a journalist who arrived and asked us for our opinion on what happened with the Twin Towers. These are ridiculous questions. The comrades called me so that I could answer the question and I told him that we are not interested in talking about the Twin Towers because we are here to do a roadblock, and if he wanted, we could talk about that.

Did you see that in the last elections, a group that calls itself the Socialist Group of Piqueteros ran for office?

You're joking!

You didn't know? There presented themselves together with the PO [Workers' Party] and the MAS [Movement for Socialism].

I didn't know that...
And? So, can we put a representative in the Senate? (laughter)

What do you all think about the issue of elections? You called for annulling votes, but what if there is a group of progressives or revolutionaries?

We say that we are a radical social movement, we organize from below and are changing the world little by little, and we would betray our values if we were to propose an electoral strategy.

We have to be clear on this point. Anyone who wants to vote, can vote; here we are not going to say "you should not vote." But, as a movement, we do not agree with voting.

There is something in your work that surprises us – you don't have a strategy for appearing in the media, for how to reference the movement.

Because we are not interested in that. In any case it depends on our agenda, not the general conjuncture. If it is beneficial to us appear in the media, or if we want to denounce something specific, we will generate an occasion to appear in the media, otherwise we are not interested.

The most important thing is to disseminate organizational experiences, not the organization's name. We are now recognized in many places, but not because we go in front of the media to mark ourselves politically to generate a following, but because we have responded to certain events and that has been noted. But we do not want to be "the" reference point.

The day that we blocked the bridges, for example, was impressive. We never imagined that something like that would happen. Later it led to a lot of things, but making becoming a reference point like that was not part of our plans, we only wanted to pressure the government so that they would feel the consequences of the repressions in Mosconi.

It was clearly an act aimed at putting pressure on the government; it was not targeted at society as a whole, nor towards the parties and organizations, because we are not interested in being the vanguard, and even less so in being part of the entertainment world.

In Research Drafts, in regards to the roadblocks, we wrote that you all do not think "from" the conjuncture, but rather that you think based on your experiences. There was a lot of debate about that, even in this workshop because some comrades raised the issue that would mean isolating yourselves from the conjuncture.

This has to do with the issue of multiplicity. We do not want to be anyone's vanguard; we want to share experiences and be infected by what is organized in other places as well. That is what we are interested in, because it has to do with everyone's cause. Not because it is politically convenient for Solano, that people organize in other places "in the same way as Solano."

For us capitalism is in the very act of thinking globally, in this way the concrete disappears. For example, there are elections on Friday and there are two ways of thinking about them: since there are elections, I have to give an opinion, or, on the other hand, based on what I am building, I will ask whether or not it is worthwhile to me, if it interests me or not. One marks their own time, there is no single place that organizes everyone's times. Nonetheless, there are comrades who organize political parties and run for office in order to fight against capitalism, but they don't have a territorial place where they build social relations that organizes their thought, but rather they think based on the conjuncture. Do you think this is the case?

This is not a finished, closed idea, but I think that, in reality, those parties are nothing other than tools of capitalism. I don't think that it is anticapitalist to organize a political party, rather it reproduces the same system. The other day we had an interesting discussion regarding children's education. We talked about how capitalism builds starting from the very core of society, from the parent-child relationship, how the conception of power is in operation in that relationship, in the idea that since I am the parent I am in charge and I have to educate you.

That is why here the children are everyone's children and we all have to take care of them. Before, for example, if a kid was playing outside, we would say: "hey, so-and-so, look after your kid." But what if that person has to do something one day and they don't have anywhere to leave their children? That is when everything started, it was in an assembly where there was a lot of discussion, and it was decided that we all have to take care of the children.

Political parties are not a result of a struggle. When I say that they are not a result, I'm not trying to say that they are dishonest. But every time I meet with a party, they say they have been everywhere: in Mosconi, in Jujuy, in Santiago del Estero. They are involved in everything! Once they tried to sell me something we had done as if they had done it. Therefore, in reality, they aren't anywhere.

They work in order for their groups to be seen. We, from below and with all the difficulties that this implies, are creating something that is real.

Therefore, I don't know if the Russian communist phenomenon was actually communist at some point, or only reproducing capitalism. Because in the end, it ended up being as elitist and screwed up as capitalism. Because when someone else thinks for you, it reproduces capitalism. It is just another name for the same thing. It is just changing the name "capitalism," that's all.

12. Organizations in struggle: coordination

How do you deal with the issue of coordination with those outside of the movement?

On the one hand, we coordinate struggle with organizations – ten, twenty, or fifty, but ones that are involved in the struggle.

The issue of hegemony is raised a lot, that no one should be able to come with intentions to assert hegemony over a struggle, to lead. Additionally, we always argue that the coordinating bodies in which we participate are not the spaces that are called upon to be at the forefront of the popular struggle.

On the other hand, each organization maintains its independence, its autonomy. That's why there was a major disagreement with D'Elía and Alderete when they wanted to assert hegemony over the *piqueterx* movement, position themselves as the leaders, because this served the system and not us as an organization.

I don't know if it makes sense to talk about levels of organization, because saying that there are levels reproduces the idea that there is a higher level and a lower level. I would speak of spaces. For example, the Aníbal Verón Coordinator is a space that was produced from a process that took years to build. It was a process of struggle, which included activities, proposals, and that eventually brought us to a place where we could say we were in conditions to form a coordinating body. I think that the most important point of agreement in the coordinator is that of respecting each organization's identity and political independence. For example, we are an organization that practices direct, horizontal democracy and in the Aníbal Verón there are comrades who argue that democratic centralism is valid. But the coordinator does not tend to form a single movement, to assert hegemony over anything, nor to form a political party or definitive organization. But it is an ongoing debate. On the other hand, the process will determine if the coordinator should be exclusively composed of organizations of the unemployed. The most important thing is that we will not coordinate with groups who want to assert their hegemony over the struggle, of who come with a dogmatic recipe of action plans, with all the steps already calculated. That doesn't work for us. We coordinate for what happens today, later time and the process, will tell.

Do you have other forms of relationship with other experiences, besides your participation in these coordinating bodies?

Yes, we have spaces for sharing experiences. That is, not only for coordinating roadblocks, but also for specific issues, questions of work, exchanging materials. For example, we have been talking to the cooperative El Progreso of La Plata about the possibility of exchanging products, and we are exchanging information: we explain how we operate and they explain to us how their cooperative functions. They have been at this for a long time. It is a type of mutual cooperation, an exchange of experiences.

Coordination does not only take place for the roadblocks and protests, it is also important for everyday life. There are university groups that can contribute something, not to our struggle, but the struggle that we are all involved in, because it also connected to their struggle. The struggle is not only roadblocks, rather it is also quotidian matters, so there is always something we can coordinate with some other organization.

13. Two forms of thinking

We do not care about who is the most presentable or who has the best discourse. When you care more about the image you present to the outside world it is likely that you already have your plan made up, a little recipe book, because it's a whole way of building a type of thinking.

There are people who work as if they had certain theoretical positions that are going to lay the foundations for their practices. When they are confronted with a limitation, they usually get stuck, and are unable to move forward.

That is, there are two different forms of thinking even within the resistance movement?

Yes, there are organizations that act as if everything were already decided, and they try to present this plan to comrades who are just starting, trying to indoctrinate them. When someone internalizes this model, they will be the militant who is prepared to guarantee the correct path.

We construct starting from reality itself, we use workshops for capacity-building in which we put forth a number that comrades bring up and we work with those, building a form of thinking that is held in common.

This leads to thinking collectively. Because you have something to offer, I have something to contribute, and together we build something new. This is like atomic conjunction: the atoms start gathering and different things start emerging, and this is a constant process.

Therefore, the assembly is the maximum expression of democratic and collective thought.

I think that these answers are never predetermined, because there is always the question; there is always the novelty.

This is very interesting because then novelty no longer has anything to do with fads, but rather is an attempt to prevent certainties from becoming become dogmas, through questioning, through making sure that thought does not get stuck or held back.

Exactly. I think that ideas are constructed through practice, based on a specific situation. Because this reality changes along with the comrades' process and that thought, which is being constructed, starts taking on a more solid shape as it transforms reality.

That is why coordination seems like a very interesting type of work for us, because it does not look for a single model for everything to follow, rather it speaks of a multiplicity of experiences, of searches and roots.

It is true that you come to more agreement with some groups, and less with others, but in all of this there is the building of synthesis. I think that all organizations, beyond the differences, the diversity, always have something to transmit, even if it is expressed in very different forms.

Because they aren't closed models.

For us it can never be closed. When we go to a meeting of the coordinating body, we don't have one comrade who goes and says what they think, but rather, they bring the proposals from the assembly, from discussions in the neighborhood. Thus, there is not a closed form of thinking there.

14. Toward an alternative economy

Have you been able to have any exchanges with the MTD in regards to alternative economies?

Truthfully, this idea of an alternative economy is very new to us. We have many more questions than answers, and we are learning along the way. Only recently have we started to discuss and practice a few things. There is the need, we have the opportunity, but we are still figuring out how to do it.

I think that we all have an idea of alternative economies. We think that it has to do with productive projects and popular education, with political education and capacity-building. This has to do with the existing, marginalizing politics and the need for an alternative, something that we have to shape from below. There are also things that we are reading or have participated in. I was just telling the comrades that I had been reading something from the World Social Forum in Porto Alegre, and there were many proposals there that had emerged from below. It was material put together by the Mothers of Plaza de Mayo and it talked about the Tobin Tax and participatory budgeting that they had carried out in a city in Brazil. But the media does not talk about these things, because they emerge from below and are things that we do; but we can't see them because the information doesn't reach us. I think that is where the alternative lies, in what is not seen, what we are doing anyways, through our creativity.

But it is important to say that we can't just make a copy, because each country has its own history. We have our own reality and experiences cannot be mechanically transferred. Furthermore, these practices take many years to develop. In Brazil, this did not start yesterday, it has taken twenty years of work, and a very specific situation, in which the Church collaborates and political parties have been able to contribute. Here there is a very slow recuperation, which is still only in its initial stages, but that shows that there are opportunities and hope. Today one cannot say that it is all a desert, because there are new experiences and new problems are arising that get people to organize.

Recently we were talking about the serious demographic problem in Solano. In ten years there will be an explosion, because there is already a saturation of families, and now there is almost no land to take over in the area. Therefore, we know that at some point we will have to leave and move toward an experience of communal life, in which we will not only seek to resolve the issue of housing, but also to develop communal forms of life. We think that this is what the comrades from the MST have done, that it is not only about taking over land in order to live, but also to produce, and anything that is missing, we will have to build. Those are long term plans.

It seems as though you see a very close relationship between the possibilities of an alternative economy and capacity-building and education.

Because if we were only to do the productive projects and not know why we were doing them, it would be impossible to keep them going. So, education has to go in parallel with the productive projects, to start thinking about the alternative that we are shaping: that there is no boss, that we are all owners of the project, why it is communal and collective, and what it means to be a collective, that there is no centralized command here, but rather we are all involved, how the coordinator works and what their role is, what it means to be organized. Thus, the two elements are both very important and occur in parallel, because it is a comprehensive project and it is about everyone having knowledge.

Often, it is not apparent what the productive projects are really about. It's not about having the money to buy a brand-new car tomorrow, but rather it is collective, communal, that has to do about solidarity among comrades, to keep going and creating other projects. But the first question when the projects are discussed is how much profit they will earn, the market where products will be sold, even who the competitors will be. It makes you ask how can they be raising these questions and not others that are more obvious. But that is what has been ingrained in people's heads and it is the first thing to appear. And they start imagining what personal issues they will resolve when they sell everything.

These are not difficult discussions, but they can tedious, because they go around in circles about issues that are not worth the time. But the comrades need time, and not just two or three hours, but many meetings.

But many comrades are convinced that salvation is coming: this imaginary has a strong hold. Or they believe that if we work and others don't, that those others are living off our work: "Why are they going to take what I produce to give it to another project?" But it gets better little by little, and many comrades are starting to understand this. Some comrades are even starting to work voluntarily, with the idea that production is not only something that is fully encompassed in economic remuneration, but that it goes beyond that.

The issue of people needing resources is a huge challenge, especially because there are situations of extreme necessity and it is very difficult to get ahead with criteria that aren't about making the most you can individually, but building a solidarity economy. But, for us, that is precisely where change occurs: when we manage to create relationships of solidarity, then we can speak of having transformed into something different.

Political education is also fundamental because ruptures always generate crisis. When you break from a life plan that has been with you since you were a child and start to experiment other forms of life, it generates a crisis. And that conflict between what we propose and what we really are is a daily conflict. Within that tension, the movement shapes a proposal: a project of living in freedom. We understand socialism as a society of overcoming, in which each individual is a complete person, but not only as an individual, but in the heart of a collective. Education is what allows us to do this, because we often encounter setbacks, in which there are conflicts in the dynamic that is recreating us. But rupture always implies conflicts, and we don't think it is possible any other way. What works as a guarantee is that we don't want to reproduce capitalism, but rather we want an economy that is embedded in a project that is life. Because it is not about how we are today, but how to develop other relationships among comrades, and that is the constant challenge. There is always tension between the new way that we want to live and the old way that we are inevitably still living.

I think that this affirmation that the challenge is to find economic responses within a comprehensively alternative life project is very important. Because what we have known up until now are two options, that are generally both failures: on the one hand, economic projects that either default or operate as any other capitalist company; and, on the other hand, political projects that justify market economic enterprises based on their stated ideology.

Listening to this, I am reminded of what Che said: "Economic socialism without revolutionary morality does not interest me. We fight against misery, but also against alienation. If socialism does not take into account consciousness, it can be a model for redistribution but never a revolutionary morality." The problem is that he was thinking this at a time when it was assumed that both things would be achieved after the triumph of the revolution. But it would be one thing to think to take office and have progressive policies and something else entirely to conceptualize an economy that is an alternative right from the very beginning.

We discussed precisely this problem in one of the delegates' meetings. There was a debate, coming from some groups that are already producing, over how the money is going to distributed. It was an intense discussion because the issue was raised that, for us, the issue of money is secondary, that first we must discuss what are the basic needs that all the comrades have. What we are interested in is collectively resolving the basic needs to live, for life; whether the issue is food, health care, or education. It is important to be able to think about the economy like that, and not in terms of the function of money or how much surplus will be left for each comrade. I think that political education is the foundation, that which sustains this new idea of not prioritizing money, because the project that we want to construct is much more important. That is what capacity-building means for us, because the life of a human and community is much broader than issues of money and goods.

Some comrades think that it would be good to take home a little money from what is sold. But I think that we have to start thinking about an alternative economy, and not about whether or not I take home a couple of pesos, that in the end does not resolve family finances or our problems as a community. I think we can resolve things through an alternative, but to do that we have to deprioritize the issue of money.

At the same time, we have to figure out how we can develop similar criteria with other organizations, exchanging experiences, workshops, what we are doing here. Furthermore, we know that an intense period is coming, there will be major austerity measures before December, and this could mean that instead of 800 people, as we are now, only 400 or 200 of us will be left. But what we achieve internally, in the neighborhood, enables there to always be a movement and something different. And this will generate support, no matter what situation we find ourselves in. The relationships that are being formed are very strong, despite the fact that there are greater and lesser degrees of commitment. There is only a small group of people that thinks in individual terms, the majority of us think in collective terms.

Obviously, there are contradictions. For example, we always say that we do not want to reproduce the boss-employee relationship, because this is not a factory. But when we are talking about people who don't show up or who arrive late, we say: "Oh right, but if you were in a factory you wouldn't be able to come fifteen minutes late. If you're late, you get fired." As much as we say this is not a factory, we still use this comparison.

And the other thing is, when looking for an alternative in order to not be exploited, you end up exploiting yourself. You supposedly become "independent," but just end up exploiting yourself.

This idea of the economy not operating in function of a life valued by the objects of power is very interesting. And it is something that is very difficult to achieve. Because it is not about making reality align with the desires of the militant's consciousness "by force," but of truly creating the emergence of other types of values and images of happiness. Therefore, an alternative economy is alternative, precisely when it is able to detach itself from capitalism's objects of desire. This is what brings about a major change: a true seed of a non-capitalist subjectivity. Speaking of all this, can you tell us about the experience of community purchasing?

What we do is group together ten families. Payments for the groceries are deducted from each *Trabajar* subsidy (which are 160 pesos each). At the moment, we take out 35 pesos since that it what we calculated for guaranteeing the basics, which includes meat, vegetables, and cleaning supplies. This is calculated on the basis of a person's weekly nutritional needs. Then, if a family, for example, has ten children and only has an income of 160 pesos, we are not going to charge them an amount based on how much they put in, but rather on how much their family needs. This is also the case for a person who lives alone and only receives what they need. The other day we were doing the calculations and I think that the person who lives alone gets about 18 pesos worth and contributes 35; while a comrade, a woman who has eleven kids, gets 120 pesos worth and puts in 35.

And there are also families that have – instead of one – four plans. They contribute for the four plans, not just for one. That is to say, according to everyone's abilities and needs.

Once a week we come together to evaluate the experience, the relations, and we rotate what we buy and where we buy it from. Our group has been doing this for three months, but now comrades in other neighborhoods want to do it too.

15. The resonance of Zapatismo and the MST

What does Zapatismo mean to you all?

I think it was a surprise when the whole world was talking about the end of ideologies, the fall of the Berlin Wall, and the start of a new era in which there would not be organizations capable of saying that this was not the case. Zapatismo was a great surprise because it helped us understand a very special moment in history with more optimism. I admired their capacity to generate an experience that was different from that which is traditionally known, something truly different. The level of participation from the communities and the capacity to shape this organization in a truly democratic way, from the heart of those communities. That is why we identify with them a lot. Knowing that a lot of work was done there, before, that is not the outcome of four or five crazy guys who came out in military gear to get people's support, but a lot of work was done previously that speaks of the movement's development and true insertion at the grassroots level and in the community.

Personally, I think we have still not fully recognized all this experience has to offer, but we identify with it because we feel that we are building a movement in the same way. Because what is seen there is the community, not an army that engages in actions that are directed toward the outside, but rather a reality to which they are intimately connected. That is what they mean when they say there is no flip side there, that nothing can be hidden. Therefore, even if we have yet to learn everything we can from those experiences, both Zapatismo and the MST are very important reference points for us.

For me, Zapatismo emerged in a moment when there was something in the social imaginary that could still not be put into words, something that we all understand but still cannot say. They were like the philosopher who is able to say it in clear and concise terms, with just the right words. That is what I think Zapatismo is, the great philosopher who said exactly how things really are, but based on concrete practices. That is what inspires admiration. They themselves say that it is the knowledge of thousands of years that they now bring to earth, a truth that has existed for a long time.

The difference that Zapatismo makes, in the political sphere, has to do with not wanting power, organizing from below, taking your time, the idea of a mandate of the majority, of truly applying democratic thought, of freedom and justice. They have also worked on the issue of dignity a lot. Then they started to show that social proposals were very important, but not the specific social proposals of one organization, alliances of organizations or political parties, leaders or *caudillos*, but rather that civil society is what is important. They even started to show that rather than fronts, it is an issue of generating a diversity of forms that can keep the struggle going, that they are all useful, it only depends on the level of participation that they generate.

This political difference stands out when they say that the social rebel will always be a rebel, which is a very important issue. Thus, it is a philosophy that starts to change the process of what, up until now, we have known as revolutions. They say that we will be soldiers to stop being soldiers, and I think what they are saying there is that taking power, through arms or any other means, is a very poor and vain idea, and that, if anything, this is a complementary idea, and not an end in itself. Therefore, Zapatismo has been like a symptom for other organizations in recent years and has started having an influence in many places. It was a means that other organizations could use to be able to grow, to take on these new forms of politics, that until that moment were still not well-defined.

Do you think that the subject of Zapatismo is very present in life of the movement? Because the MST is talked about a lot and you can tell it is very present.

In the movement in general, no. It is sort of what happened with Che, that Marcos's photo is recognized, or a song like that of Ismael Serrano. Here they take some phrases and some stories. For example, in several workshops they are working on the story about the lion and looking-glass. But the influence is not as strong as that of the MST, perhaps because we have had more contact with people from the MST, and we do not know Zapatismo from within. But smaller groups of comrades have gone into their writings in more depth.

What about the MST has interested you the most?

Recently, we were in Córdoba with comrades from the Association of Producers of the Northeast of Córdoba (APENOC), and they commented that they had held an encounter about the issue of land with people from Mexico, Brazil, and other places. We know that it is possible to articulate all these struggles on many levels.

From the beginning, we have taken a lot from the MST, especially the issue of popular education. Some of us have taken courses. And also taken things from their mysticism (laughter).

For example, from the MST's seven organizational principles, we take three: horizontality, direct democracy, and autonomy.

And you weren't in agreement with the other four?

They have things about forming cadres in three levels, this is not something we use. Then there is the issue of the leaders' insertion into the masses and we do not have leaders, here we are all on the same level, so there is no insertion to think about. And then there is the issue of the historical subject, which is a whole other debate.

16. Hypothesis on counter-power

How do you understand and practice what we have come to call counter-power?

We feel like since the beginning of our experience we have raised issues in a way that coincides a lot with what we have shared with you all over the past few months. The decision to stop repeating patterns from the past, without denying their usefulness, without saying that it was all done in vain, but rather trying to grasp the immensely positive elements of historical experiences. But in this situation where we find ourselves, we would have to be a little crazy to try to create a popular organization, from below, for social change, that is meant to overthrow the political power of capitalism. This is something that leads to a crisis. For example, not all the comrades see it this way, because there are many recipes that have been repeated, which gives them strength.

But today the movement is walking a different path. I think we have had the intuition to say that this is not a matter of four crazy people who got together one day and said let's build a movement like this, but rather we have also proposed to recreate ourselves, to subject ourselves to change as well, as we have thrown all our certainties out the window. Now we are in this situation that is being built. All of this has generated a lot of uncertainty because it is a different way of building a movement from what we are used to. We are usually very structured, so to say that this is being built, with a ton of questions for which we still don't have answers, generates crisis. But it also gives us the humility of knowing that we don't have to know all the answers, because history has also shown us that knowledge can be oppressive, that the one with knowledge is often the one who dominates. Counter-power is built through these experiences in which we are no longer oriented by a struggle for political power, regardless of whether or not some comrades in the movement today do not accept that; it is something is still be debated.

We have a plenary session on Friday in which we will present a more detailed document with the organizational forms that we work with. We have held several discussion meetings in the neighborhoods and what comes up is confirmation of the commitment to a movement that not only struggles for economic issues and subsistence, but that we are convinced that it is the seeds of a new society, in which we will overcome all of the bullshit we have in our heads, like selfishness, etc. What emerges with considerable force is the fact that we are not interested in taking power, nor in disputing political power, but rather starting to live as we have often dreamed. And the time is now; we aren't going to have to wait for a revolution, or for major world transformations, rather we can already start to live like this and apply these values.

For us counter-power has to do with autonomy. And we still don't have complete autonomy as an organization, but are moving in that direction. We already know that because of the current economic crisis, much of what we have achieved now we won't have next year. This brings challenges, creativity, and lucidness.

It is very important to recognize that it is not about transforming the municipal government, or the police force, among other things, but rather that these things exist today as things that we no longer want, we reject them, we negate them. We don't want to substitute any part of that system, we want to build something different. And it is that new thing that we are envisioning, constructing. That is counter-power.

Today we were asking ourselves: how do we relate to comrades who used to be in the movement and then left because they were not interested, or because they do not agree with the MTD's criteria? How can we continue having a relationship with that person? Because they are our neighbors, and perhaps we have the same dreams, even though we have different ways of reaching them. I think that counter-power also has to do with that, with being able to accept difference, and to be able to live together based on that diversity.

There is something that the Zapatistas say: we do not want to change the world, but rather to create a new one.

I think that it also has to do with a term that we use a lot in the movement: social change. We have started to see that this change will be not be achieved by a political party, by an alliance of organizations, or a proposal that comes from up above; but we are also seeing that there will not be only one method, but rather thousands of social forms. But nor will they be specific social proposals, belonging to a certain sector. For example, we participate in coordinating bodies but these coordinators are not our representatives, but rather spaces in which all our voices, their multiplicity, are expressed.

I think that these are the things that sometimes set the MTD Solano apart, because little by little it is marking a revolutionary path, but different from what we have always called a "revolution."

This is what is seen in the roadblocks when comrades grab their sticks and cover their faces, they recover that internal flame that is dignity, that has to do with this new path that is being made. That is what happens in the roadblocks, although the media only shows it as flashes, soundbites.

It is clear that the media does show the alternative of counter-power. They are not interested in it. Therefore, every time we give a talk, we start by saying that we are more than what the media portrays us as – masked people on the streets, burning tires, social renegades – we have something more important to show: this whole thing that we are building, this whole social project that lies beneath it.

The other day a comrade asked me how we understand the issue of strategy, and I responded with precisely this about building the base, the problem of regional autonomy, and that we don't propose a unified central power because that would be exchanging one power for another. And he responded: "That is utopian." And when we asked him, who says that it is utopian, he said: "History says so." But we are also history. Perhaps that is what the history that has already happened says, but the history that we are writing right now can say something else. Many, drawing on the manuals, say to us: "How can it be? There is no party or leadership. You are making a mistake." "You already messed up" they said to us. We are going to build something new, maybe we are making a mistake, but perhaps not. But, what is the point of creativity if we aren't going to use it?

We don't want to leave anyone behind. We have many comrades who have been destroyed by this society: years of misery. It's easy to get angry about so many vices, egocentrism, selfishness; but these comrades are victims of the system. We believe that the new generations, the children of the comrades, will be more complete. That is also part of the work; it does not end with us. Here we are making a great effort to create counter-power, but we do not have the full plenitude of our freedom; this is our limitation. We are leaving something for those who are coming, and perhaps they will be able to carry forth what we ourselves cannot do.

Once a comrade asked: "And if a popular government comes to power, what would we do?" And an old Paraguayan brought up the case of Salvador Allende in Chile and the problems that he had. The question was would our attitude be in that case; there was a debate over whether we would make them appear like good politicians: if we would support them, collaborate, or what. Reviewing the idea of counter-power, what we said is that we would continue doing what we are already doing: it is not our goal to have comrades occupy political office or take on the government's responsibility, but rather that the organization must continue as alive and vital as it is now. That is, there would be no reason to dismantle the organization if a popular government comes to power. And many comrades did not agree with this. But we insist that that best role that we could play as an organization is to not dismantle ourselves, because even if the government has good intentions, we should not lower our guard: organizations are the best guarantee for it being a truly popular government.

It would be like in the Brazilian states in which the PT wins, if the MST were to disintegrate and stop taking over land. The issue is what would happen if the PT gains power on a national level, whether it would ask the MST to stop. I think the same thing would happen that happened with Villa and Zapata. It would stop being a popular government; if it was a truly popular government, it would not order popular organizations to stop organizing.

17. Elements for evaluating the project of thought-building with Solano

For us, these months of workshops have meant finding many elements of the work that we are proposing. We think that the fundamental requirement for knowledge today is developing a situational form of thinking, a knowledge that emerges from experiences of creating new forms of life. And if this workshop has been anything, it is precisely a very powerful experience of collective thinking.

I was recently rereading some of your things, especially the booklet on MOCASE, and I realize – personally – that I had dissociated the intellectual from the practical. The issue is that I see many comrades who start to think and write without it having anything to do with what is happening, with what is being built. For me, the workshop helped me understand the meaning of thought-building, of ideas, of understanding in this respect, a meaning that empowers practice.

It always bothered me that many people belittled the work that we were doing: "the unemployed who block roads," they would say. But I had not fully recognized the importance of what we were doing either. Through the debate, it became clear that what we are building is something much more important than what I thought. Not thinking that we are going to change everything, but that is where the debate about multiplicity comes up: being able to take on multiplicity as a form of construction. *What has happened to me is that I can no longer imagine my life without you all. To me it seems that it is simply about finding ways to continue working together. I have discovered that we are the same, because we are in different places.*

We did not have a space to talk about ideas because of the rhythms and demands of daily life.

I think that here we learned something that we had said before, but without having had the experience: the possibility of moving beyond political articulation, of working without plans or programs. Because I think that this is a space that functions without everyone remembering exactly where everyone else is from. That way each group does not only leave with what they already had, but it produces something more, something beyond a sum of the parts. Therefore, these types of encounters generate bonds and relationships between very different experiences, that refute the conception that dispersion is the only alternative to traditional political articulation.

Notes from the Workshop

1. Summary of the workshop on June 12, 2001.

Project Intentions

We think that this first encounter went really well and was an excellent starting point for our collective work. We outlined a space based on trust and a community of searching, in which we propose to collectively analyze the problems, obstacles, and characteristics of a new form of militant experience. There are some questions we should keep in mind and clarify, so that we can build this space of production and investigation on solid ground.

First, it is fundamental to be able to think together. We are referring to a form of conversation and encounter around a common fabric, organized around the problems that brought us together. The group's common project is thinking about our problems, inventing possible solutions, or – at least – ways of posing the questions that open up new perspectives. It is not about coming to agreements between different "positions" or opinions, between different people or groups, but of reaching a state of contemplation that allows us to start seeing things, theorizing problems from a point of view that we could not reach in any other way.

This is very important: it is not a matter of "agreeing" about a "new theory," or "incorporating a new language," but rather being able to think about problems in order to give them a new practical perspective.

This work that we are doing together, these workshops, must lead to the production of materials that can circulate and contribute to political education. For this to happen, we think that is not about insisting on and circulating what we already know, but rather that we must begin to think about things that truly enrich our practices, based on being able to bring up issues that would not have come up any other way. This means that we are not motivated by the objective of meeting a predefined goal, but what matters to us is the possibility of a real experience in common, that will create challenges and require certain discipline. Therefore, it is fundamental that we are able to prepare for the workshops, and take the time and make the effort to address the concerns that seem essential to us.

Summary of the conversation

The jumping off point to open the meeting was the proposal to think of the differences between the figure of the "revolutionary" and that of the "social rebel," a distinction formulated by Subcomandante Marcos. It attempts to account for the emergence of new type of militant, committed to social change in a concrete way and through the work implied by this objective. Marcos said: "Their fates are different. The revolutionary tends to become a politician and the social rebel never stops being a social rebel. The moment that Marcos or the Zapatistas become a revolutionary project, that is, something that becomes a political actor within the political class, the Zapatistas will have failed in their alternative proposal. A revolutionary fundamentally proposes to change things from above, not from below, the opposite of the social rebel. The revolutionary says: we will make a movement, take power, and changes things from above. But not the social rebel. The social rebel organizes the masses and starts transforming things from below without having to posit the question of taking power. Politicians are needed, unfortunately, but what are especially needed are social leaders. I think that Zapatismo should and will opt for being social leaders..."

In the discussion some very powerful ideas were presented based on the experiences of the MTD-S:

In the current struggles, we are experiencing a form of understanding emancipation according to which, first, it is about having a very clear idea about what we don't want. We have confirmed – based on concrete experiences – the problems of all the politics that have been tried up until now. In those forms of politics, socialism was a pre-established model that they tried to "apply" to reality and power was the place from which to threads of society were controlled. Thus, power occupied a central role in the revolutionary conceptions of classic socialism.

Now we have to assume that there is no previously laid path to follow. Now, for us, it is about making new paths as we walk and effectively explore these paths that we are opening. This means constantly creating new forms of organization, thought, and life in the midst of the very real experiences that we inhabit.

Thus, collective work becomes crucial, the concrete construction of a community, as a truth in practice and a form of decision-making and thinking. Accordingly, an authentic idea of democracy begins to emerge: democracy as a necessary and everyday practice and dynamic, and no longer a way in which state power legitimizes itself to the people.

It is a question of "organizing rebellion," the rebellion that already exists and constantly grows in the face of the system's injustices. Rebelliousness is not a characteristic of individuals, but rather must be collective.

However, it was also specified that rebelliousness alone is not enough to explain our struggles, but additionally, and fundamentally, it is about affirming another society in the present, and not only negating power.

Here the different visions regarding the experience of the roadblocks, emerges. For some comrades, what is fundamental is accumulation in order to blow up power, for others (us), the work that needs to be done is different.

We constantly find ourselves pressured by the need to have things resolved and then we run the risk of acting like the traditional left, always trying to "express our ideas." Militants start to have crises, provoked by the uncertainty, by the sense of stagnation that seems to characterize this form of building. On the one hand, we constantly demand "results" and on the other, we live with many types of uncertainties.

Finally, it was proposed that the movement's guarantees are, fundamentally, constant rebelliousness, popular participation, and the construction of basic agreements about how to work together. Later, a hypothesis was proposed that was based on research carried out by Colectivo Situaciones in Moreno[15] and that consists in distinguishing between three forms taken by popular solidarity experiments.

This distinction seeks to differentiate between when a collective experience is merely circumstantial and when the experience produces and affirms a new subjectivity or social relations. In reality, this distinction never exists in a pure state, but rather is always expressed in gray areas, in which elements of the three become mixed.

A first level includes experiences in which the groupings occur in function of individual interests, of "momentary" demands that are not satisfied. It is an issue of solidarity with those who are excluded or going through a "difficult time," but that, strictly speaking, what they desire, what they "hope for" is to escape this situation. There, solidarity lasts as long as the situation of exclusion. Later, since they aspire

---

15   The investigation took place over a number of months, and was developed along with various alternative groups in Moreno, including the Los Horneros squat and the educational community *Creciendo Juntos*. Some aspects of issues raised in this investigation, in particular the long and interesting interview with Creciendo Juntos, can be found in the publication *Rough Draft of Investigation*.

for inclusion, the solidarity experienced during "difficult times" simply remains a fond memory.

These experiences are very temporary, not because of their duration, but because they are conceived as a resource necessary "as long at the problem lasts," but not as a place for the insistence on the positive creation a new form of sociability. For these types of experiences, struggles are a means to a concrete end: inclusion or satisfying specific demands. It ends up being very easy for governments to manipulate these experiences and they don't constitute a real threat to dominate social forms. Nonetheless, these experiences sometimes "derive" into higher levels (at least in regards to "new sociability").

A second level consists of experiences sustained by the convictions and actions of militants. This includes groupings (alternative schools, popular education groups, community kitchens, roadblocks, or anything else) that attempt to sustain their struggle solely based on the will and consciousness of their members. Here ideas of change and forms of organization and struggle appear that attempt to overcome the channels pre-established by the power structures. "New forms" or "alternative forms" always emerge from these experiences with the goal of "constructing new social relations." But they are highly dependent on the militants who sustain them. Additionally, a major problem of these experiments, which are almost always very valuable, is that they are sustained by a group's will to "construct" the new sociability, as if this could be planned based on consciousness and/or theories.

Lastly, we confirmed the emergence of experiences of popular organization that start to show elements of a non-capitalist sociability. It is no longer a matter of "because we are bad off, we are going to get together and fight to be included." No, these experiments start to affirm different ideas of life, of happiness, of political organizational, of ways of funding them that no longer seek "inclusion." Therefore, here we speak about a "new sociability." That is the foundation of counter-power.

Unlike the second level, in which the militants go about "applying themselves," according to their good will and what is dictated by their conscience (or their pride or political party), this counter-power is not based on what "a group wants," but rather there are hundreds of experiments that are reaching similar conclusions, beyond what a particular group of militants, intellectuals, or leaders says. The elements of a new sociability are not created by anyone in particular. They emerge: they are created by people in struggle. Counter-power does not have an author (or authors).

It is about the historic appearance of a new subjectivity, new forms of thinking, raising and resolving problems of existence. We think that we are entering a new period, in which the figure of the individual, the foundation of capitalism (and historical determinism and the myth of progress) is in crisis, and a counter-power is emerging, a bond between people, among the experiences that create another sociability in practice.

In these experiences, the militants are no longer those who "know" about the "model" of the coming society, nor those who desire power, but rather those comrades who are committed to thinking and working *from* and *for* experiences, in strengthening counter-power and making it visible.

This hypothesis becomes even more important if we take into account the difficulties that counter-power faces in the neighborhoods of the Buenos Aires urban periphery, where the destruction of community bonds, lack of trust, disputes over power, and individual solutions predominate. Counter-power thus faces enormous difficulties in affirming itself as a new sociability.

Here we see the difference, for example, with the Zapatista movement. There, in some ways, the Indigenous community (pre)exists, with its forms and customs, and resists the society of individualism and capitalism.

In Buenos Aires, popular organizations and communities have been destroyed, and there is no other subjectivity to grab hold of than that of capitalism. It is the organization, then, that starts to recreate social bonds, at the same time as it carries out a demand-based struggle. Therefore, the levels are often mixed: the demands-based struggle, the importance of the militants in the experience, and the construction of non-capitalist relations of solidarity for the base (the base, for us, is the only thing that exists. We continue using the image, but should clarify that investigating counter-power, there is nothing other than the "base").

A new sociability and a new subjectivity cannot be created in one day. It is a long process that has already begun, and not a question of the voluntarism of a group of militants, intellectuals, or leaders.

One of the major challenges lies in making sure that the dynamic of the popular organization predominates over the "militant who provides solutions." In this sense, the MTD-S has managed to establish an interesting dialectic between the objectives given and the real experience of neighborhood residences in their process of struggle and discussion.

Another concern that has appeared has to do with the creation of spaces of encounter. The question of creating spaces in which the collective and solidarity are not a means to another end, but rather the very essence. Or, in the same vein, going from being "neighbors" to being "comrades."

The roadblocks, as such, are no longer a novelty. Now it is clearer that what is powerful is what is left from and in the roadblocks. What especially stands out is the camaraderie and mutual respect produced by the struggle in the roadblocks, moments in which everyone's fate is tied together. In those moments, social bonds are reinforced that organize and encourage commitment from participants, imposing discipline and a form of operating collectively.

We have managed to collectively approach "core ideas that are more productive politically" that address problems of life as a whole and not only the question of the benefits packages (for example, the fight against leptospirosis).

One challenge the movement faces is that of making "qualitative leaps," in other words, that the comrades who are joining the movement grow as people, which implies that they start taking up the values and meaning of the movement. (Here we can see the extent to which the movement constructs subjectivity, in the same way that it carries out other tasks without which that work could not be done, which seems to be characteristic of counter-power).

The idea is that they be able to perceive that organizing is not only a good way of obtaining benefits packages, but fundamentally a new form of life. It is about expressing one of the movement's principles that indicates there is no hierarchy among comrades, that the spokespeople are not foremen, and that wages are not a cause for submission.

The "qualitative leaps" are absolutely linked to capacity that must be achieved in the encounter between new comrades and spokespeople.

On the other hand, the qualitative growth of the movement is tied to the ability of the work spaces and different levels of the organization to function well.

It is essential that their functioning continue to improve (from organization and security in the roadblocks to the productive workshops, from educational spaces to the pharmacy, from the coordination with other MTDs to the commissions of each neighborhood).

On another note, we do not want to grow "too much" or agitate "excessively," at least until what is already being organized functions well.

We also talked about the importance of the relationships we have been building with neighborhood residents who are not members of the movement. There has been a consolidation of the movement. There has been a reconciliation of family relationships that had crises because some family members participated in the movement while others rejected it, fundamentally because of the campaigns to disparage the movement by traditional institutions of power in the neighborhood. These attacks have decreased in the face of evidence that participation in the movement is growing and increasingly considered legitimate.

"Implicit solidarity" is starting to be deployed (neighbors are no longer denouncing the movement, and even silently collaborating). Perhaps this is not spectacular but it is decisive, especially when it comes to recomposing and building new social and community relations. One comrade told us about a conversation he had with a neighbor who "condemned" the movement's activities, in which what he did was "tell the neighbor what it is we do, and not what he, the neighbor, should do." This example demonstrates the *potencia* produced by the movement in its everyday activities.

Lastly, we spoke of the implications of the politics of counter-power, of the concepts that that it proposes and the practices and thoughts that it produces. We spoke of the difference between counter-power and the idea "building popular power." These are very minor differences, in the sense that they are differences between comrades with very similar lines of thinking, and things inevitably get mixed up all the time. The main difference is that popular power puts the issue of state power in the center, and, from there, it proposes popular power to reach it. On the other hand, counter-power starts by removing the state and its administrative apparatus from the center of our problems. The consequences of "removing the state from the center" are quite large.

To mark some of these differences, we can see, for example, that there is a different idea of the subject and its relation to power. To put it briefly, counter-power is based on the *potencia* of the specific situation in which it works, in the experiences in which it participates, and only trusts in this work located at the grassroots level. In that situation, the elements for its construction are already given, and there is nothing to wait for: neither taking power, nor building the party, nor anything else.

Thus, the problem of power is displaced from the centrality that it has had historically. Additionally, the idea of power is different: counter-power's struggle is not only against central power, but also powers as such and how they act in the situations we inhabit. Primarily because domination is not a distant phenomenon, but is reproduced in the most everyday actions, from what is desired to how relationships are understood.

The struggle against power is posited in two ways: against the domination of the state and of the market. Popular power only attacks its global, solid, external existence. But counter-power recognizes that the market and the state start with us, that their foundation and their force is not mythical, but real, with deep anthropological bases. Therefore, if we do not produce values that are superior to those produced by capitalism, we will never change social relations nor start to think differently: we will eternally reproduce the same powers.

We can summarize this difference by saying that while building popular power is a just political position, counter-power does not privilege the political over other elements of life. Counter-power implies a path of creation, in which there are many problems that do not "have" pre-existing solutions. Some of these problems, that remain pending for future discussions, include:

The type of relationships, bonds, which are necessary in order to build with different experiences of struggle;

The relationship with state institutions and subsidies;

The characteristics of our own management areas that we are creating.

Nonetheless, and despite everything that was said, we spoke of how it is not helpful to treat the contributions from different revolutionary movements throughout history as "old, useless, rags" and to "throw the baby out with the bath water." We also addressed the issue of the identity of unemployed "workers." The MTD defends this identity and does so by postulating that it emerges from the fact that we are productive subjects (and therefore workers) of life and not as people whose identity is shaped "by" and "for" capitalism. Life, then, is much more expansive and essential than what capitalist production and alienating demands impose on us. We insisted that work involves the people's productive and creative *potencia*, and is not a "classification," a label, that defines us more than our actions, impoverishing us.

Another issue that remains for another conversation is thinking about some fundamental lines of thought in regards to the meaning of "the death of historical determinism," a central idea of capitalist modernity, that has also influenced experiences of emancipation. For example, the very idea of reason and knowledge, of the evolution of history, of totality.

2. Summary of the workshop on June 26, 2001

In the meeting on Tuesday, June 26, we discussed the popular uprising in General Mosconi, in the province of Salta. Comrades who had participated in the uprising were present at the meeting. A few points emerged that we can work on in the following encounters.

We started by reading out loud the document that summarized what was discussed in the previous meeting. There the discussion about the figure of the "social rebel," proposed by Subcomandante Marcos in opposition to the revolutionary, emerged again. It was clarified that it is not a problem of naming, nor of language, that the words can be used interchangeably, as long as we are always clear about what each of them means. The idea is to think about the existence of a new type of militancy, that acts from below to permanently transform the conditions of life and that, in contrast to the traditional militant, no longer prepares for forming a political party nor to reinsert struggles in the logic of "building-taking-winning power." Marcos has – like all of us – a discovery in his hands: change not only comes from below, but also, the way to ensure that change is not only temporary, also lies in grassroots struggles.

Therefore, it is not a question of forming organizations that are only, or mainly, in dialogue with the state, but rather the most important thing becomes the movement's capacity to address other struggles and people working for social change.

Resonances of Salta

Interesting things emerged when discussing the consequences of the struggles in Mosconi: The extent to which that experience did not produce the emergence of a "new political group" became clear, but nor is it simply about a "sectoral struggle."

A "new political group" tends to represent the movement of struggle and "represent them" to the government, political parties, and the media. Ultimately, all of the energy that was unleashed in the struggle ends up in negotiations with the state (whether the provincial or national government). At best, this leads to more or less concrete gains. At worst, the group benefits at the cost of the community struggle.

A struggle that is simply sectoral leads to a similar result.

The experience of General Mosconi shows us that the struggle is taken up by the entire community. The process has great legitimacy because the whole community joins through a concrete struggle that people highly identify with. Thus, it is an intervention that does not take up the traditional forms of what are typically considered "political" struggles (sectoral demands or party struggles for power). Therefore, it is difficult to "identify it." This is especially true for governments, political parties, and the media, in other words, for those that tend to put labels on things and construct the images that circulate socially and politically. Later, we discussed the spontaneous self-organized mobilization that took place in Solano in solidarity with the struggle of comrades in General Mosconi. The mobilization came out of identifying that struggle with "our cause," that is, confirming and feeling the relationship that existed between the different experiences. This is a case in which "one" mobilizes because of what happens to the "other," but it is no longer an issue of solidarity between two separate situations, but rather between experiences that participate in the same reality. We are not referring to the existence of direct bonds between the experiences, but rather at the level of resonances, with the way in which struggles that take place thousands of kilometers away are immediately taken up as one's own.

This in particular enables thinking about the nature of relationships between experiences of counter-power. These relationships are no longer only created by agreements between groups. It is not like in capitalism in which people only understand each other through the existence of mutually beneficial contracts. What motivates a struggle is not the profit calculation, but rather the evidence that the fate of our struggle is tied to the fate of those other struggles. Organizational forms are envisioned and put into practice as a consequence of that, and not as a precondition for solidarity. This is very important, because it shows the extent to which this is not only about a conjuncture, or a more or less coincidental moment, but rather a degree of maturity of a sociability that is attempting to give birth to a figure that is superior to that of the "individual." It is no longer that type of solidarity that someone who is better off than "that poor one" who is worse off, but rather a practical, immediate solidarity that does not require long speeches to exist materially and, above all, is no longer ruled by calculating the political profit.

There is a clear difference between this mode of solidarity and that which is practiced by political parties and (advanced) union federations. These apparatuses move over struggles, attempting to "represent them," and determining what it is convenient for them: they only take concrete steps depending on their usefulness for the accumulation of their respective organizations. But if this does not occur, if there is nothing to accumulate, or if "the profile doesn't fit," they begin to hesitate and when the struggle becomes difficult, they vanish.

What happens with these organizations is that their decisions are always guided by a search for consensus. Their whole practice can be explained by the search for majority adhesion (but, as we know, the majorities do not exist in themselves, but rather as an inert representation whose name is used to justify positions). "What would the 'majority' of people say?" They don't stop to think that people do not think the same when they are alone and demobilized as when they are committed and involved in struggles. Thus, it is impossible to be in agreement with those who "don't do anything" and those who "are working all day" at the same time, since those are two different positions. You can't both seduce voters, TV spectators, that whole mass of people who lives their daily lives submersed in individualism and, at the same time, those who participate in activities, who work against selfish and market tendencies.

They remain tied to the "logic of power," which is exclusively concerned with "the majorities." Therefore, they are not free to do what they "would have to do" if they were free.

The organizations that always speak to the state and the "majorities" forget to address the enormous masses of minorities that are struggling against the model of power and oppression here and everywhere. Therefore, they lack the freedom to act as they "should" (which is a matter of producing forms of life that escape the current sadness). Renouncing that freedom is very serious. That path does not even produce mistakes from which we can learn: mistakes are sources of knowledge when there are movements of free men and women to learn from them.

Returning to the experience in Salta, there was insistence on one important difference with respect to the MTD of Solano.

Because, at first glance, you could say that these are two "piqueterx" organizations and thus lose sight of the fundamental differences between them. One of these differences between the two circumstances is especially important because it demonstrates the specificity of the movement building that takes place in the urban periphery of major cities (especially Buenos Aires). In General Mosconi, and in many experiences that have unfolded in the country's poorer provinces – in contrast to what might be assumed – the community dynamic is much stronger. In those places, they have maintained traditions and customs that keep people a little safer from capitalist degradation than in the more developed cities. In the words of a comrade who visited and experienced Salta: "perhaps the comrades in those roadblocks do not have such an enviable organization, but they are much better mentally and emotionally."

In Buenos Aires, on the other hand, social bonds have been very destroyed by the logic of the system, and, therefore, the responsibility and necessity of the organization becomes that much greater. Especially in terms of something that already came up in previous meetings: the importance of spreading values that reconstruct sociability. Building social, personal, family, political relationships, ultimately a subjectivity of struggle, of community, of the project, is at the center of the movement's work.

This is the truth that escapes those who think that the roadblocks in themselves are "a form of doing politics" that "is convenient now," or that it is a "fad," which is one of the things we need to dig deeper into. In Salta, as we were saying, the whole community quickly identified with the struggle of the *Unión de Trabajadores Desocupados* [Unemployed Workers' Union, UTD], which led to the organization's decisive importance, and its weight, it is not as notorious as in Solano.

The media's attempt to use the deaths of two comrades to break the movement failed precisely because of that community dynamic in which the whole town took up the struggle as its own. So, when the government sent its emissaries, the first thing that was demanded was the release of the comrades who had been detained.

Summing up, in Solano the organization has to take up the work of rebuilding the social bond destroyed by the effects of a system of domination and impoverishment of all people.

A question was then raised: Is the lack of a well-structured organization in Mosconi a problem or not? Is it a deficiency, or simply a different form of subjectivity that works with organizations that are more suited for its ends, to its circumstances, and, ultimately, a different experience?

With respect to the MTD Solano's organization, participants shared its history beginning with its foundation. They recounted its birth and fundamentally said that the important thing about this process is the consciousness of the extent to which it is a form of struggle for which there are no models to follow. Instead, it is about generating spaces in which new social relations are instituted. Organization posits, then, a problem and necessary moment but in conditions in which there are no models, doctrines, or recipes.

Another problem perceived by the comrades who were in General Mosconi was the UTD's relative isolation in relation to other movements of the unemployed. For the UTD, at least up until now, establishing links with other experiences does not seem to be a priority, although due to what happened, it remained open to the possibility of constructing more fluid exchanges.

We discussed what a relationship between such different movements would look like and said that it should be based on a concrete practice, looking for what both situations have in common, beyond the particular characteristics of each expression of struggle. This way of thinking contrasts with that of party militants who tried to tell the comrades from the UTD what they should be doing.

Another topic that was spoken about was violence. What caught all of our attention was the subjectivity that is constructed in these experiences. Violence is just one more element of the struggle. When it comes from below, it is defensive and expresses popular outrage. It is violence that responds to the violence of power.

We also talked about the phenomenon of the roadblocks and how they have become generalized as a form of struggle, especially after their recent repercussions. It was said that Mosconi marks a turning point, in the way that it demonstrates the depth of popular struggles. We also said that we have to be creative, to not be pigeonholed. Breaking things is not always the answer, neither are roadblocks; and there we could see the difference with those see the struggle as having other ends. The criteria that are taken into account when planning a roadblock are the result of previous discussions and everyday collective construction. The form of the blockade depends on the tactic that is deemed most suitable to achieving the specific objectives. For example, when addressing the problem of leptospirosis, it was an issue of denouncing (and pressuring) the municipal government. Therefore, we blocked access to Solano and the government had to respond by creating the necessary sanitation conditions. In the case of solidarity with the comrades from Salta, we sought to block a neuralgic location, as a way to pressure the government so that it would withdraw the gendarmerie and to have an effect in the media that would clearly show our solidarity with the comrades. Whenever we plan a roadblock, we keep in mind proximity to the neighborhood in order to not be isolated.

These sections of the conversation demonstrated that where political bureaucrats only see a "sympathetic tactic of struggle" – which is also spectacular because of its radical nature – there is a collective and everyday project of building a new life. Where some see a mess that is necessary to materialize their political plans, there is really an alternative construction.

State benefits and alternative economies

In the second part of the meeting, some of the main problems facing alternative experiences were addressed.

The issue of state benefits and subsidies was raised as a discussion topic. Based on the specific experience of Solano, it would be interesting to analyze if these subsidies benefited popular organization or if, to the contrary, they limited its development and potential. Colectivo Situaciones recounted two visions that appeared in their research in Moreno. The first takes the benefits as a "revolutionary tax" that must be charged to international capital and that is useful for developing and strengthening the organization. The second position, to the contrary, sees the subsidies as a factor that paralyses struggles, co-opts its leaders, and neutralizes autonomous productive strategies, putting the process of community organization on the back burner.

Strong doubt emerged in the conversation about whether or not the *Trabajar* benefits could be incorporated into the organization as just one more element or if the organization's fate depends on them, thus making them a dangerous factor. We said that three levels must be taken into account in regards to state subsidies: first, the subsidies have to do with subsistence, since in most cases, the 160 pesos from the benefit package is the family's only income. In this sense, it was said that "without the benefits, there would definitely be much fewer people in the movement." On a second level, we have the solidarity contribution made by members to sustain the movement. Here a first element of solidarity appears. The percentage of contributors is very high: 90% of people who receive a subsidy contribute ten pesos to the movement.

We are also starting to work on transforming the "solidarity work" that is carried out to "justify" the benefits to the government, into autonomous productive projects. It was recognized that there are important obstacles regarding this objective and that, in turn, it is a fundamental challenge for the movement in its struggle to achieve real autonomy from the state.

The issue of the function of the subsidies, then, appears to be very closely tied to the possibility of initiating autonomous productive strategies. For the comrades, these strategies should be alternatives to market production. Not only because market relations are antagonistic to the values that motivate us in militant construction, but also because of the issue of concrete effectiveness: today the market is not a means for satisfying the needs of residents of Solano. There are ideas and projects that we are attempting to develop in this regard. It is an issue of taking advantage of the quantity of hours/people of existing work (of which there is are a lot) in the production of non-commodities, in products for our own consumption, directly linked to residents' needs. It was said that, despite the impossibility of controlling the whole productive process, since the materials for production have to be bought in the market, if we manage to produce and establish a system of exchange that eliminates profit – that is, in which prices equal the input costs – it would be possible to even double the minimum wage, no longer in monetary value, but in products and services.

Here a topic emerged that is difficult and concerning for many experiences of counter-power: the relation between these alternative productive enterprises and the macro-economy. In many of these cases, they have been able to get ahead in economic terms, but at the cost of delays or direct death of the political project. In other cases, staying faithful to the political project means the economic projects fail.

There is a very important issue that is directly related to these projects: for the majority of neighborhood residents, it is impossible to think about (and act in) the economic dimension in a way other than that imposed by capitalism. We talked about the lack of a "culture of work," understood as a form of socialization and relationship that characterized the workers' movement. In the province of Buenos Aires, chronic structural unemployment has caused the acute destruction of bonds and the ethics of cooperation and living together. This is translated into the daily impossibility of maintaining minimum work discipline.

Nonetheless, the true obstacle seems to be the difficulty in breaking with the conception of work as a capacity that is sold in the market, that is, as something designed to produce profit. Thus, all the productive activities that are not ruled by these criteria are not considered work. Work tends to be understood as making products, that can later be justified to a bureaucratic government administration or sold on the market. What is needed, therefore, is the creation of a new conception of work and this seems to be a slow and difficult subjective process. However, it is a priority. We also discussed the difficulties in overcoming dependency on a boss. It is very difficult to overcome the need to be directed in order to produce.

Multiplicity and Counter-power in the Piqueterx Experience

Colectivo Situaciones

1. The roadblock as a precedent

The *piqueterx* struggle emerged outside of traditional political and social institutions. Its autonomy and novelty are related to traditional political institutions' loss of prestige due to their incapacity to reshape the conditions of domination of so-called late capitalism or to produce lasting changes to improve the living conditions for the majority of the population.

The roadblocks are a mode of struggle that brings together those who were expelled from the factory centers: the unemployed seeking to resolve problems connected to their own existence, reorganizing themselves territorially in places where the most difficult battle was that against the dissolution of social bonds. From a structural point of view, the roadblocks are a consequence of the decomposition of the country's industrial base.

The *piqueterx* are currently returning to many of the elements and the knowledge of the labor movement from earlier decades – the "picket" itself is taken from "factory pickets." But this methodological prolongation was not taken up automatically and mechanistically, but rather transformed under the new condition of being "joblessness." This precise point marks the elaboration of a legacy rather than the passive acceptance of an inheritance. What is at stake here is the subjective *potencia* of the roadblock, in terms of the ability to invent forms of struggle based on establishing a situational sovereignty.

In effect, it is this elaboration that enables the roadblock to think from a *singular place*. From there, the *piqueterx* operation consists of establishing a complex relationship with the state apparatus and recreating new modes of inhabiting the territory – the neighborhood – reformulating, in an innovative way, its relation with the labor and union tradition with which it undoubtedly has connections.[16] Among these shared aspects, there is one that should not be underestimated: both unionism and the *piqueterx* movement have had to invent forms of struggle that are capable of altering normality; they have had to create concrete forms of making themselves heard. If the worker is able to interrupt the productive cycle through a strike, the roadblock takes on its essentially territorial condition by blocking the circulation of commodities through a simple and audacious direct action: blockading the roads.[17]

Horizontally organized, their form of working and decision-making lies in a state of permanent assembly. Their origins are recent. They emerged in the mid-1990s in the country's interior and spread across the country in less than a year. The deployment of roadblocks energized the participation of the unemployed in struggles throughout the country in a movement that spanned from the interior to the province of Buenos Aires. This velocity of the socialization of the roadblock overflowed all the state's forms of co-optation and repression.

The media baptized them as "piqueteros," producing a stereotype. Later, diverse interpretations came into play and the figure of the "piqueterx" emerged. In its dominant version it is a description determined by the place that they occupy in

---

16 The *piqueterxs* are not a direct continuation of unionism. Their foray into social struggle in Argentina makes it necessary to open our eyes and analyze the specificity of their presence and its effects. It is true that there are lines of continuity between the two, but it is also clear that the conditions and precursors are very different. In any case, union movement's attempts to extend its control and forms to the roadblocks have been a source of conflict. There are elements in the roadblocks that cannot be reduced to any will to subsume their singularity in systems of different practices. Furthermore, the deterioration of union structures has not escaped the perception of the roadblock. While, in its origins, unionism consisted of a form of collective association aiming to reinforce the autonomy of the working class's cultural experience, later the role of union apparatuses changed radically. With the arrival of Fordism as a method of organizing production, there was a profound modification in the character of those organizations. The mechanization of work and the institutionalization of the wage relation as specific mechanisms of domination led unions to become the transmission pulley of power in relation to the working class, coordinating its incorporation into the state and destroying its experience of autonomy. The roadblock can be understood, better yet, in relation to the initial unionism, as a mode of socialization in which knowledges and victories are shared, establishing communitarian social bonds.

17 The roadblocks do not exclusively inherit knowledge from labor struggles, but also more recent struggles. Since 1993, there has been a series of insurrections and *puebladas* [uprisings of entire cities or towns] in several provinces in the interior of the country. The roadblock appears as a higher level of organization of the unemployed and contributes to channeling those struggles. The roadblock is the weapon of those who have no resources other than their capacity to control territories with their presence. In this sense, it is the common patrimony of the unemployed, the Indigenous, the evicted, and a broad conglomerate of people that neoliberalism calls "the excluded."

the social structure: "excluded," "without work," "victim." This "piqueterx position" emerged from associating the condition of abandonment with a single methodology: the roadblock.

But as the "piqueterxs" started speaking for themselves, the extent to which "piqueterismo" group together a multiple and heterogeneous variety of experiences became clear. There were even attempts to unify the whole movement – which was essentially multiple – under the naive pretense of homogenizing and institutionalizing it. All of these attempts have failed.

The *piqueterx* movement is a true *movement of movements*. As such, it has produced an authentic revolution in terms of the collective perception of popular capacities for creating new forms of social and political intervention.

2. The conjuncture and different ways of thinking

The National Piquetero Congress was carried out in the first half of 2001 and was a key moment in the construction of the movement. Practically all the *piqueterx* experiences from across the country were present there. Its – partially achieved – objective was to give birth to a national coordinating body. The proposal: to bind together *piqueterx* heterogeneity on the basis of a relative community of demands and forms of struggle. Immediately a shared action plan was approved that had a twofold effect: it demonstrated the force of the *piqueterx* struggle, the justness of its demands, and that it had achieved an advanced level of organization, as well as making visible, for the first time, the different ways of conceiving the struggle.

Two distinct positions, with different forms of thought, subsist in the movement. On the one side, there are the more structured organizations (mainly the *Federación Tierra y Vivienda* (Land and Work Federation, FTV) linked to the Central de Trabajadores Argentinos (Argentine Workers' Central Union, CTA), the *Corriente Clasista y Combativa* (Class-based and Combative Current, CCC), the *Polo Obrero* (Workers' Pole, affiliated with the Workers' Party) and the *Movimiento Teresa Rodríguez* (Teresa Rodríguez Movement, MTR)), which operate based on a form of thinking that derives its premises from terms of "globality." "socio-economic structure." and "conjuncture." It is based on terms of "inclusion/exclusion." Their positions are not homogeneous. They are traversed by the traditional axis of "reform or revolution." On the other side, in the less structured organizations, the panorama is not any less heterogeneous. The experience of the MTD of Solano can be grouped among the latter, as well as those of other movements that make up the Coordinadora de Trabajadores Desocupados-Aníbal Verón (Aníbal Verón

Unemployed Workers' Coordinator). These experiences base their thinking on expanding the bonds that constitute the materiality of their experience. Thus, they distance themselves from the classic terms of debate between reform and revolution. This operation is characterized by self-affirmation and practices of counter-power.

With the generalization of the *piqueterx* phenomenon, political organizations assembled their apparatuses for facing – co-opting or combating, according to the cases – the crisis situation. Traditional or leftist parties, churches, and unions became aware of this movement and approached them with the intention of capturing their *potencia*.

The media have contributed to making the movement accessible. They show the *piqueterx* struggle as subordinated to the coordinates of the "political and economic conjuncture." The *piqueterxs'* struggle loses all of its singularity and becomes an element of "another" situation, which is more important because it is more general: *the national situation*. The *piqueterx* struggle then ceases to be, in itself, a situation with which to commit oneself, to be become just one more actor, another element, of the *general situation*.

However, accepting the inevitability of the point of view of the *general* implies, at the same time, subordinating all situations to a mere portion or segment of a totality that is always already constituted. This way of thinking constitutes a subjectivity that physically and affectively separates itself from the situation, taking it as an object and relating to it in a purely analytical form. This rationality speaks to us of the prudence with which each one of should choose our options, since it is no longer only about piqueterxs – that were transformed in "a part of the whole" – but rather, precisely about the good of that "whole" – "the country," "the common good." etc. Abandoning all specific responsibilities, they abstractly take responsibility for the luck of governments.

The concrete operations of thought distribute positions within the *piquterx* movement. Where do you start from in order to analyze the situation itself: from the situational concrete that you inhabit or from a hypothetical – and not always materialized – national situation? Where do you start in order to produce the experience's *meaning*?

If we accept the premise of a form of thinking that abstracts concrete conditions from its intervention and extracts its meaning from a general situation, we arrive at a subjectivity governed by the temporalities and requirements of the *political conjunctures*. On that path, the piqueterxs are forced to derive the motives of their struggle from the meanings available in the totality in which they work, taking up a rationality conditioned by forms of socially instituted legitimacy.

Meaning is shaped for the struggle in the debate: *inclusion* or *revolution*. The first argument says: the struggle is legitimate because it does not demand rights other than those that emerge from the fact of being part of the whole – citizen, worker, human being. The struggle for *inclusion* is the struggle for recognition. It is about being admitted as a part that legitimately – and legally – belongs to the national-state whole. This form of obtaining legitimacy takes an indisputable premise for granted: that the nation-state maintains its ability to integrate and that political struggle consists of going from *exclusion* to *inclusion*.[18] In this analysis of struggles, the piqueterxs who adopt that perspective abandon any pretension of *imposing* their terms onto the rest of those who make up the society that they want to be part of – the non-piqueterx population. This creates a struggle over the tensions and majority opinions to define the terms of democratic inclusion. The premise is formulated, then, as the existence of a democratic state that is able to exert its integrating powers based on consensual and representative principles.

The second argument, the *revolutionary* position, declares the need for social alliances with the objective of conquering state power. The roadblocks that adopt this position take themselves to be the *revolutionary vanguard of the Argentinean people*. The social totality will be transformed by forcing a change at the heart of social organization by taking control of the state apparatus. The expectation is focused on the possibility of the parts of social whole recognizing the roadblock as a true representation of that social whole reconciled with itself: the *piqueterxs* as the new proletariat, the subject of history. This position shares a common premise with the previous one: social classes acquire their meaning based on their economic being and they aspire to social change through state powers.

Situational thought acts on the basis of other premises. Class, clearly, exists. But its economic existence is not enough for giving rise to social change. What is needed, above all, is to affirm situational meanings to create social change; that is, to activate the production of values of a new non-capitalist sociability. Thus, counter-power distances itself from the general term as a provider of meaning, to affirm a radical and irreducible point of view. The situation is not perceived as part of a whole, but rather as a concrete totality that is not passively subordinated to any abstract totality. This distancing opens the doors for a subjectivating, ethical process of re-encounter with *potencia*. This path, obviously, sidesteps the traditional polarization between "reform and revolution."

3. Representation

---

18   This position can be identified with the thesis held by the CTA and the FTV.

Within this polemic, the question of "representative politics" plays a central role. The call to unify the *piqueterx* movements brought updated this debate. The position calling for unification proposed a complex operation: to make the movement's multiplicity into a unity that could be represented as such. To be able to be represented, the One must be constituted as such. Multiplicity was perceived more as an obstacle than as a source of *potencia*, or, in any case, as a source of *potencia* to control. This affirmation was responding to questions about how to make that *potencia* become a determining factor in the general situation, or how to transform that *potencia* into a "social-political" force that would be able to directly influence the national situation.

These questions speak to us of a hegemonic will that starts to experience multiplicity as a dispersion of forces. Suddenly, what had been seen as a source of *potencia*, becomes a major obstacle. How to build a finished representation of the multiple? How to build leadership, a leader, and a single discourse on foundations that are so unsuitable for that operation?

The leaders of movements that insists on that path, were effectively entering difficult terrain: their decisions to be increasingly mediated by the complexity of the conjuncture, their aspirations, and the need to sustain the movement. Along the way, their relationships with the base of the movement were transformed.

Political representation condemns those who posit this operation to an irremediable exteriority with respect to the forces that express themselves at the movement's base. This exteriority emerges from their role as *administrator* of those energies.

In the specific case of the National Piquetero Congress, the positive and negative elements of that position became apparent: on the one hand, strengthening the capacities of a clearly defined movement to achieve concrete gains with regard to their shared demands towards the national government. But, on the other hand, having a handful of leaders take up representation and leadership in the name of the entire movement weakens the *piquetero* movement in two ways: it liquidates the multiplicity within it and grants the leaders a disciplinary authority toward the rest of the movement. This authority consists of the power to determine who is a *piqueterx* and who is not, what is the correct way to act and what is not, etc.

This complex mechanism was put to work during the first day of action of the protest plan called by the First National Piquetero Congress. The then head leader debuted in his role by denouncing those who chose to radicalize the forms of struggle as "not belonging to the movement." Once this operation – of transforming the unrepresentable multiple into the represented One – is carried out, the *piqueterx* phenomenon is revealed/betrayed: it is only an actor in the political conjuncture. Its rationality is determined by its economic interests. Thus, its efficacy is reduced:

from the *potencia* of a multiple struggle to the capacity of its leaders to act as "valid representatives." The initial multiplicity becomes a predictable "actor of the conjuncture." The success of this operation would now depend on new factors, such as "containing" the action of *piqueterxs* according to the objectives established by the movement. Two different logics appear. The leaders think on one level, the grassroots on another. And the fate of the whole, it is said, depends on the movement adapting to the perception of the leaders. These objectives on which the success of the movement depends start to be played out on in purely super-structural level of action. It is not that there are no longer assemblies or mobilizations, but rather that they are re-signified by a meaning that escapes the members of the movement and is only fully understood by its leaders.

The political importance of this operation tends to be underestimated. But it has very material effects. When the movement takes on the image of its leader, that leader stops being a spokesperson, one face among many, to start acting in the name of a "general *piqueterx* will" that he or she interprets. This happens independently of who the representative is. The exercise of representation disempowers the represented. It divides in two: the represented and the representative. The representative calls the represented to order, to be able to exercise their office. The represented, if they are docile, if they don't want to the relationship with representation to fail, should "let themselves be represented." In that way, the representative administrates the relationship. They are the active part. They know when mobilization makes sense and when it is better to stay calm. The representative tends to expropriate the sovereignty of the represented. Forget the mandate. The mandate starts to bother them. It becomes an obstacle to their cleverness.

After all – the representative feels – he is the one who has to work in a place that the represented are not familiar with: *political power*. The representative has, in effect, a *vision of power*. He goes about getting to know power, learning. He becomes, for everyone's good, the teacher of the represented. He explains to them what they can and cannot do. He acquires particular skills, and starts to get the represented to agree with his points of view. The representative is thus able to construct his own mandate, taking into account the role that corresponds to the represented: to be *his* base. When this happens – too many times – the struggle loses its radical nature. The representative becomes *rational*, but it is a rationality that is incomprehensible for those who share the experience of struggle: *his thought is no longer collectively constructed*. The represented no longer think with him. The assembly ceases to be an organ of thought to become a place to legitimate and reproduce relations of representation. The representative constructs an apparatus for controlling the assembly. It becomes a plebiscite. People vote on options, but those options are constructed beforehand.

All this does not mean that representation is inevitable, nor that representation will necessarily separate into an element of domination. The delegate with a specific revocable, rotating mandate, *who thinks in – and with – the assembly*, and does not crystallize into a permanent figure, has no reason to separate from the whole. Or, in any case, if they do separate it does not put the organization in risk, since nothing has been delegated to them, other than a specific mandate. The key to this question is avoiding that representation becomes independent, something that happens when one thinks in terms of power, when one separates themself from the situation of concrete thought, from the experience from which they emerge.

Thought that extracts its own premises from the conjuncture leads to a form of existence that is overdetermined by representation. Only when this operation is successfully carried out, does it open the conditions for negotiation, for the *inclusion* of the *piqueterxs* in the institutional dialogue that is opened by the force of tricks and maneuvers, ultimately, the consensual game of the political system. This whole development is tied to a politics of *integration*.

4. The inclusion of the excluded... as the excluded

For this operation of representation to be possible, it is necessary to have previously recognized a common property among the represented. From that determination, they can be spoken of – in their name – in a recognizable, in other words, *legitimate*, form. Thus, the dialogue constructed by the representative requires, as a necessary condition, the pre-existence of a defined social group based on shared characteristics: the workers or the unemployed, students, the excluded, whatever. It is a matter of the complex problem of *identity*.

Identity can be deduced from a structural property of the existing group, that is, based on a more or less sociological category – such as the unemployed – or it can emerge from the creation of a new term, which cannot be deduced from already constituted identities. This is what happens with the identities of rebels and insurrectionaries. Identity is produced through a name that is associated with a subjectifying act.

In the first case, the name, the identity, the representations that surround the group, saturate and objectify it. Sociological categories condemn these subjective forms to act – like in a play – the script imposed the structure of the roles. How do you *become* an unemployed, an excluded – a *piqueterx*? What appearance is adequate? What is the language of those without a job?

The category of the unemployed does not manage to capture the radical nature of the *piqueterx* experience. The path of representation reduces all of the struggle's experiential multiplicity. All the situational richness is, from that moment, subjected to a process in which the intensities of the real, of the lived experience, are lost. The movement becomes reduced to a place of passiveness. The unemployed have to fit into a pre-existing image: an unemployed person is someone who is looking for and wants, more than anything, a job. They want to work, not *question wage society*. They are missing something in order to be complete: they are the *excluded*. Their complaint is transparent: not having access to the labor regime.

In contrast, the *name piqueterx* expresses something else. *Piqueterxs* speak to us of a subjective operation. It is not synonymous with the *unemployed*. The unemployed is a subject determined by necessity, defined by a need. The difference is enormous: the *piqueterx* has been able to produce a subjective operation over a socially precarious foundation. They cannot deny their condition, but nor will they submit to it. In this subjective *action,* they appropriate their own possibilities for action, of subjectification. Nonetheless, the "piqueterx" has often been used merely as another name for the unemployed. Those analyses do not capture the subjective potential of the piquete. These are perspectives from the outside, even if they are taken up the unemployed themselves. The piquete is defined as an act of hopelessness carried out by "victims" who do so in order to survive. This makes the piquete seem like an automatic reaction. It depoliticizes it. It ignores the experience of the *piqueterx* organizations themselves. It denies their character of insubordination and their creation of an alternative sociability. Like the worker, who automatically goes to the union when suffering a pay cut; the unemployed, a step lower on the social ladder, on the other hand, run to the roadblocks. As they cannot go on strike, they invent the piquete. It is nothing more than that: social automatisms.

This is how the representation of the paradoxical figure of the *excluded* is constructed. Because the *excluded* is not really such. *Exclusion* is the *place* that our biopolitical societies produce to be able to include people, groups, and social classes in a subordinated way. In the words of Agamben, the excluded is *the name given to the included as excluded.*[19]

Contemporary political thought builds on notions of the *excluded* and *included.* The former participate in the social body under the miserable mode of only being subjects of – economic, educational, medical, etc. – necessity. Their action is so

---

19   Giorgio Agamben, *Homo Sacer: Sovereign Power and Bare Life.* Stanford: Stanford University Press, 1998.

mechanical that it cannot even be considered action at all. Rather than an action, all their activity is nothing other than an illusion. Real activity is that of a cause and effect type: the causes come from need and the effects from desperation. There is no thinking or ethics to their actions. As such, all the actions of the excluded can be explained a priori: they are about demanding goods and rights, which any observer would immediately be able to deduce. An excluded is a being with deficiencies, who, by nature, demands inclusion. That is all.

The politics of integration is based on this distinction between *inclusion* and *exclusion*. It announces its prescriptions based on the assumption of the premises of such a distinction. Thus, it is a matter of threatening the regime based on the desire of *inclusion* of millions of *excluded*. This pressure is paradoxical. Because once it is understood that *inclusion* and *exclusion* are places that pertain to the same society, then it must be recognized that exclusion is the concrete and historical form in which a set of people are included in this society, and in no way is it about people who are outside of society.

Nonetheless, the illusion of inclusion is believed to be able to exert pressure that will generate benefits. At a minimum, those benefits include further-reaching integrationist social policies, or, at most, it causes a crisis in that society that functions based on that hierarchy of places.

The first case does nothing but strengthen the places of *inclusion* and *exclusion*. In the second, in contrast, the operation is very different: *inclusion* is demanded precisely when such *inclusion* is impossible, in a way that would demonstrate the lie behind the discourse of integration that conceals the biopolitical separation of the social body. Asking for inclusion – economic, political, social – is asking for the impossible, at least under the conditions of neoliberalism. Thus, they believe they are carrying out a subtle operation in which a politics of radical transformation is concealed beneath a universally acceptable demand. The *potencia* of such a politics is rooted in the legitimacy that it obtains. Its advantages would emerge from three features. First, it would be carrying out a politics of rupture under the form of an inclusive politics, that is, it would go beyond inclusion. Second, this going beyond would have the legitimacy of the discourse of inclusion. Finally, this politics offers valid interlocutors to power in times of chaos, which always gives it the possibility of obtaining resources.

There is, nonetheless, an objection that might challenge a good part of this argument. It is that sometimes there is a supposed anachronism in this line of reasoning. Exclusion is not part of hegemonic politics. There are no promises for the excluded. What is strengthened by demanding inclusion is the position of exclusion and this does not weaken in the slightest the apparatus that separates ideological places of "inside" and "outside." *Inside* and *outside* are not, then, objective places within a formal structure, but rather an ideological spatiality that is useful for processing contemporary forms of domination, distributing people in separate sites. Thus, there is fierce competition among the included. Not only against the other, but also – and especially – with our very selves. It is a matter of increasingly assimilating to what is prescribed by the norm of inclusion. Exclusion, on the other hand, is nothing other than the "low" form of inclusion. This topological structure, however, is not organized according to a dual logic, but is *fractal*. Like the ying-yang symbol, both poles live in the space of the other: there are peripheries in the center and centers in the peripheries.

The risk, then, lies in polices that, claiming to create a rupture with this spatiality, end up reproducing it. While they claim to make exclusion disappear, in practice, they affirm that place of the excluded, contributing to producing the figure of the poor. The concrete risks of politics that think in terms of inclusion is rooted in the "inside" and "outside" pair, while simultaneously forgetting that exclusion is nothing other than a subordinated inclusion of the excluded as subjects that affirm need. This is what causes movements shaped by the ideology of integration to lose their radical nature.

5. The political illusion of *piqueterx*

If the politics of inclusion means accepting one of the main premises of the current mode of power; the politics of rupture carried out by groups that maintain the line of taking central power shows us how *political illusion* operates within *piqueterx* groups. These groups affirm a traditional revolutionary position.[20] They postulate more radical methods of struggle and announce a non-mediated confrontation with power and security forces. We said above that this current demonstrates the same tendency as the "inclusionists" to think on the basis of political conjunctures. This methodology has three fundamental components: class, the program, and the strategy for taking power.

Especially since the events of the 19th and 20th, this tendency assumes that

---

20   We can identify these positions within the Piquetero Block that emerged as an alliance bringing together different currents on the movement's left. Among others, this included the previously mentioned Polo Obrero (Partido Obrero) and the Movimiento Teresa Rodríguez (MTR), as well as the Movimiento Independiente de Jubilados y Pensionados (MIJP), Here there the Movimiento Territorial de Liberación (MTL, tied to the Communist Party), and the Movimiento sin Trabajo Teresa Vive (tied to the Socialist Workers' Party).

we are experiencing a situation mass social uprising and a profound crisis in the power bloc. This is what has traditionally been called a "revolutionary situation." Based on this reading of the conjuncture and their own conceptions of social change, these currents believe that it is the moment to constitute a revolutionary political vanguard to direct struggles. This operation consists of entrusting the more combative *piqueterx* groups with the task of representing radical struggles. They believe that there is the capacity and opportunity to create a "qualitative leap" that would allow for going from dispersion to the synthesis of popular struggles under their leadership.

The *political illusion* does not consist of a delirious reading of reality, rather it is an option of thought that consists as much of deriving concrete lines of work from general analyses as a determination to politically force a situation that is incapable of problematizing the concept of revolution. In effect, the illusion of rising to power to then change things from there has immediate consequences in everyday practices. The "political" times of an accelerated conjuncture force and disorganize the times belonging to situated constructions. Militant efforts begin having abstract objectives. Discussions about prioritizing objectives are regulated according to increasingly general criteria. Little care is given to the experiences seeking to produce new social relations and everything in the movement is recentralized in the name of the "serious" work.

This impossibility of subtracting oneself from the times and demands of the conjuncture weakens work at the grassroots level. It is increasingly difficult to discover spaces of open reflection. Confrontation thus stops being a requirement of struggle to become the "highest" moment. Organizational hierarchies are justified by the same requirements of the political conjuncture or because they end up thinking, as a famous *piquetero* leader is said to have stated, "only grass grows from the grassroots." This path also generates a distancing between the leaders and the collectives that produced them.

Grassroots work is seen as transitory, initial experience lacking in political density. The movement is built on "levels" with advantages for the professionals in conspiracy. The social movement is often forcefully substituted with political apparatuses and all faith is placed in the coming of a political supplement. All militant agitation is left waiting for the messianic "leap" that would position the movement in the struggle for power.

6. From multiplicity to counter-power

The biggest difficulty for the National Piquetero Congress consisted of the questions of *unity* and *organization*. From the beginning, the issue of organizational forms had been fundamental for the radical movements working on the grassroots level. Dominated by assemblies, commissions, discussion groups, and horizontal forms of decision-making, the movement's multiplicity is not synonymous with disorganization. To the contrary, it is characteristic of the combination between its multiple being and its high level of organization. These features are not exclusive to each experiences of the movement, rather there are also highly organized coordinating bodies that respect the movement's heterogeneity at the regional and national levels. And the same goes for the level of its leaders. Understanding the roadblock in terms of its specific *potencias* means comprehending its singularity. *Piqueterx* leaders are more effective if they operate within the assembly and the coordinating body, than when the separate from those apparatuses to chase after public opinion. In fact, their leadership consists of their capacity for contributing to maintaining situations of thought along with their comrades, collaborating to develop the *potencia* of the experience. Outside of this concrete situation, the *piqueterx* struggle has no interest.

The strength of the piquete does not lie in the demand for inclusion. As the members of the MTD Solano explained, it is not a matter of "getting back inside." It is known that there is no desirable "inside." To the contrary, positioning yourself as "wanting to enter" means joining the line of those who shape their subjectivity based on having a place in sociological studies, in the discourse of power, in the archives of the ministry of social action, in the plans of political groups or NGOs.

The *potencia* of the piquete, the hypothesis is, lies in the movement's capacity for subjectivation that exceeds its character of the excluded, the poor, or the unemployed. Its singularity speaks to us of a dignity of insubordination and the exercise of resistance as the creation of sociability.

7. Thinking of the radical nature of the struggle

Subcomandante Marcos would say that the *revolutionary* is characterized by the struggle for power oriented toward the future society; while the *social rebel* – the Zapatista – feeds the rebellion daily in their own circumstances, from below, and without believing that power is the natural fate for leaders. For the Zapatistas, it is clear that all situational action must subtract itself from the traditional axis that polarized between "reformists and revolutionaries." In turn, the extent to which both positions hide the same image of *power* and *politics* becomes clear. They both postpone the *potencia* of popular struggles and present the same difficulties when it comes to working in immanence to the situation.

Marcos's social rebel does not think in terms of the global, but based on *singularity*. It is a strategy for thinking that affirms its capacity by putting *globality* in parentheses. It is the philosophical difference between the abstract universal and the concrete universal. There is no naivety: it is not a matter of negating conjunctures, but of thinking of them as elements internal to situated thought. Radical groups, such as the MTD of Solano, call this capacity *autonomy*: thinking with their own heads and in function of the concrete situation. This implies knowing how to ignore the *external emergencies* projected by media circuits and militant micro-climates, in order to re-encounter their own capacities for understanding and intervening.

Radicalness, then, does not consist of the infantile negation of reality, as claimed by the *realist* critics of counter-power. To the contrary, it is about thinking in terms of *specific comrades' concrete actions*. There is already a battle over the *quantification* and *instrumentalization* of experiences and struggles contained within these excessively simple formulas. Radicalness is the effective capacity to revolutionize sociability by producing values that overcome the society of the individual. This option, in the case of the MTD of Solano, also implies investigating the movement's forms of organizations, the possibilities for enacting an alternative economy, the developing of capacity-building and popular education, the type of relation with state management, etc.

Additionally, this modality is especially suited for understanding the forms in which the issue of violence appears in the *piqueterx* movement. It appears on at least two levels. The most obvious is the roadblock. But there is also the violence of the person who has decided to begin resisting against current forms of domination. These levels of violence do not maintain much relation to the traditional forms of political confrontation. *Piqueterx* violence is not conceived as a political strategy for taking power. It is not a tactic designed to impact public opinion, but a secondary and inevitable derivation of a form of resistance.

Thus, the picquets take up violence as an element of struggle that is not, nor does it become, the fundamental act. It is just one more element in a multiplicity, when it is conceived as a *decentralized practice* and a legitimate form of *self-defense*.

8. The case of the MTDs

If the experiences of the CTA-FTV and the Piquetero Block have allowed us to analyze a form of thinking and working within them, we can take up the experience of the MTD Solano in the same way, as a practical modality and a different way of thinking. The movement's origins can be found in the church of Solano, Quilmes. They were evicted from there by Bishop Novak. Later they started organizing the MTD Teresa Rodriguez[21] in collaboration with similar organizations from Varela. The movement's force began to intensify when they managed to administer their own projects, through the *Trabajar* benefits packages. They quickly established commissions and political education workshops, a bakery, iron-working, training, popular education, a movement pharmacy, among other projects. Their roadblocks could immediately be distinguished by several characteristics: the social representation of the neighborhoods where they work, the extent of the mobilization, the use of face-coverings, and the particularity of their blockades.

The comrades from MTD Solano participated in the First National Piqueterx Congress. They participated convinced of the need to nationally coordinate the struggle and not be isolated in the face of increasing repression. During the gendarmerie's repression of *piqueterxs* in Mosconi, in the province of Salta, MTD Solano took part in roadblocks cutting off access to the city of Buenos Aires in solidarity with their comrades as the repression continued. Nonetheless, they took part in the Congress with little enthusiasm. By then they knew that their focuses differed from those of the three convening forces (CTA, CCC, and PO). However, they were excited about the delegates from the interior of the country and, in general, the combative climate that took over. During the first day of action, they observed how the majority forces attempted to shape the movement. One episode from those days demonstrates the positions at stake: on the first day of the action plan, in August 2001, the MTR occupied a bank, demanding paychecks that had been delayed. This action had not been agreed upon by the coordinator, which immediately created a dilemma for each movement that had been present there.

The MTD Solano decided to abandon the coordinating body with the MTR due to their lack of consultation, but, at the same time, they stayed there to guarantee a rearguard. While they were there, however, they were surprised by the reactions from the rest of the movement. As the rest of the coordinating groups started denouncing the MTR, the highest leaders of the *piqueterx* movement spoke to television and newspapers denouncing members of the MTR for wearing masks.

---

21   The MTD Teresa Rodríguez split in 2001 between the movements that continue working as an MTD and the previously mentioned Movimiento Teresa Rodríguez, MTR.

Three days later, the leaders of the MTR were arrested in another occupation of the labor ministry of the Province of Buenos Aires. This situation coincided with the second day of action. The MTD Solano then decided not to participate in the mobilization to the Plaza de Mayo and mobilized to La Plata to demand the prisoners be freed. On the third day of action, they stayed in their neighborhood resisting the auditors that the government had sent to detect "irregularities," which would allow them to suspend the social benefits packages.

In the following assemblies, the members of the MTD Solano discussed these issues. Upon reflection, they felt that their strength did not lie in positioning themselves in the conjuncture in competition with other *piqueterx* movements, but rather in prioritizing the construction of a counter-power, from below and according to their own possibilities. They decided, then, to focus on strengthening every project, every commission, every task, every activity in the neighborhoods. It was neither a matter of *localism* nor a lack of perspective of what was happening in the country, or in the world: when the repression took place in Salta, as we saw, they immediately took to the streets. Nor is it a useless isolationism, but rather a necessary *delinking* from the logic of globality.

That same methodology orients the way in which the MTD Solano takes up their relationship with the – national, provincial, and municipal – governments. They administer social benefits packages granted by the government without this meaning any type of capitulation. They simply understand that a process of situational affirmation implies a complex relationship with the state. And in that process, they express their own knowledges of social change and revolution. These knowledges address the complexity involved in receiving funds from governments and, at the same time, establishing high levels of confrontation with them. Agreements and confrontations, nonetheless, do not exhaust the links between the MTD and the state. Additionally, there is the autonomy of thought and action that brings them to organize an alternative economy to sustain the movement when the benefits eventually stop.

Social change, then, is aware of these three tactics or forms of relation with the state. Each of them corresponds, in turn, to the very nature of the current state. On one side, it is a disarticulated nation that no longer has the monopoly of political legitimacy over the national territory. On the other hand, it is a state that has been co-opted by market forces, which frequently leads to violent confrontation. Finally, it is the representation of capitalist hegemony that exists at the grassroots level, with which autonomy is the only guarantee for developing non-capitalist tendencies in the political conjuncture.

Meanwhile, they are not naive in regard to the state's repressive functions, therefore autonomy involves internal work about the character of the coming confrontations. Along this line, autonomous popular organizations – not just *piqueterx* organizations – are learning increasingly effective forms of popular self-defense. Constantly seeking to not become isolated in the face of repression is another way in which situational groups recognize the conjuncture: always in function of their own needs and circumstances.

The MTD's lines of development are prolonged in the work of the coordinating bodies. The MTD Solano worked within the Coordinadora de Trabajadores Desocupados Aníbal Verón up until 2003. These are encounters in which the territorial movements do not dissolve, but rather resources, knowledges, and mobilizing capacity are strengthened in the face of specific circumstances.

9. Identity as creation

We have seen how two different ways of thinking have different results. There are no practices without ideas. Thought materialize in practices, to the point of not being able to differentiate – other than formally – between thought and practice. The first form of politics exalts the existing structure of society, precisely as it is represented by the analysis of the conjuncture and discourse of power. The identities of the worker, the unemployed, the poor emerge mechanically from the social, productive, or distributive structure and subjects each worker to their classification – role – of worker and reminds each unemployed person that they are "without work." Multiplicity is lost. And with it, the strength of identities of struggle. As we said above, this is not the only way of thinking about things, even if it is the dominant way, and thus seems natural.

In fact, identities constructed in struggle function precisely in the opposite way: instead of expressing those who are pigeonholed together in the battered social structure in the conjuncture, the structure itself is deconstructed. They are designations that identify the multiple and not a property that produces an alienated subjectivity. Thus, the identity of the insubordinate always involves a re-creation, a resignification. Workers usually struggle for – and with complete justice – higher wages, or in opposition to those who would cut their wages. But *workers* as a radical category struggle against the *wage relation itself*. The unemployed fight for more employment, for jobs, to enter the productive structure. When that doesn't occur, they fight for unemployment benefits. But the *unemployed* who we are talking about here, the *piqueterxs*, struggle against the society of alienated labor, individualism, and competition.

The *piqueterx* movement is still being constructed. It is a movement of insubordination, but also of the construction of new social relations, of counter-power.

The consistency of the figure of the *piqueterx* as insubordinate or as a social rebel, however, is *fragile*. This fragility is not because of its youth, but rather due to depending on a fragile free spirit from the moment in which it does not develop from any place of power. It is a *fragility* characteristic of counter-power itself, that pursues the line of *potencia* through investigation, thought, affect, and the production of new knowledges of emergent social protagonism.

The 19th and 20th and the temporalities of the movement

MTD Solano

On Monday, December 17, we initiated an action plan to face the repressions that we knew were coming: we called for more unemployment benefits, for on-time payments of benefits, for food, and health care. It had been decided, in the coordinating body, to carry out a powerful action against the private sector. Therefore, that Monday, we surrounded eight supermarkets in the area of Quilmes, making our demands and proposals. The action lasted all day, and there was a response: at least the national and provincial governments acknowledged the action, it hurt them.

At one moment, we crossed a line: comrades hung from the wires because the owners were not paying attention to us. They communicated with the government and pressured them to respond to us. The supermarket gave us just four hundred kilograms of yerba mate. But they threw the ball into the state's court. "We are not doing well," the supermarket owner told us.

The *piquete* at the supermarket is not only about obtaining food; it goes much further. This allows us to reflect and delve upon what it means for us to attack a multinational corporation, and not go out to protest without knowing the difference between looting a supermarket and looting the neighborhood corner store. Before and after going out on an action like this, we needed to dig into its meaning with our comrades: why does this action go beyond the issue of food? This enables us to think about how we sustain our struggle.

That week caught us in the middle of an unfinished action plan. What we had achieved was a promise for food aid and to pay us on time, but nothing concrete. On Tuesday, we had decided to attend a conversation with the national and provincial governments, to evaluate the results. On Tuesday, December 18, they signed the agreement so we stayed in our territory. That night, looting began in San Miguel, in Moreno, in the province of Entre Rios and we saw how the unrest was growing. They had promised us that the food would be delivered on Saturday and they sent it on Thursday, December 20, which caused a mess because it was at the height of the looting. The night of Wednesday, December 19, mobilizations started in the neighborhood, there were rumors of looting, directed toward supermarkets. When our comrades came from the different neighborhoods to pick up their food, the police got more intense and started shooting. The previous day had already been heavy, since the declaration of the state of siege: threats, rubber bullets, in some cases, arrests, pursuit.

On Wednesday we went to the plaza with a group of comrades. The state of siege generated a lot of contradictions for us, it was in the middle of an action plan and we started getting ready for serious repression. At that moment, we thought that the state of siege was planned to repress us and other organized sectors of the population. In fact, today we are evaluating whether things would have been much worse for us if the middle class had not gone out to protest like it did. When we saw what was happening in the capital, some of us decided to go. When we arrived, there was already repression in front of Congress and people had been injured. We reached Congress around 1:30, and people had dispersed. Then we decided to go to Olivos because we heard on the news that something interesting was happening there, but when we arrived nothing was happening. Ultimately, we came back and started talking among ourselves about what was happening and the idea emerged in the assemblies to do something territorial, here in Solano, because of the police repression.

On Thursday, we had to go get the comrades out of jail and you could see that many groups of young people had been detained. That is, not only had they repressed people who were organized, but the entire neighborhood. The idea was to scare the neighborhood, to stop people from going out to protest, from going to the Plaza. In the afternoon, we watched as the situation developed in Plaza de Mayo and there, we changed our thinking; it seemed that the territorial option was not the way to go, but that it was about the Plaza, where things were happening. We held assemblies in the neighborhoods where we could. We explained that the situation was very complicated and that anyone who wanted to participate should be aware that things could get nasty. Thus, about seventy of us went to the city, in a bus that we found. The police were not letting people leave the neighborhood, and when they saw groups of people walking in the streets, they arrested them. We lost a lot of time trying to figure out how we could get out of the neighborhood. Comrades from other organizations called to warn us to be careful because they were stopping people on the bridges. So, we went very modestly. When we arrived, it was a disaster.

The closest that we got to the Plaza de Mayo was one block away. But something funny happened when we arrived: when we came out with masks, we were quickly identified as *piqueterxs*, and comrades who were fighting with the police became more courageous and started throwing rocks at the police, with a lot of intensity! So, for us, as soon as we got there, the repression started, the police on horseback, the tear gas. We did not even have time to think about what to do. That was the first retreat, we didn't even have time to organize a barricade. It was all very abrupt; it took us four or five blocks to come together and organize ourselves. We resisted for several hours.

Things started popping off on 9 de Julio Avenue and they started shooting us with lead bullets. They kettled us, we had to get on a bus and try to get the driver to get us out of there. Other groups stayed and we met up with them here later. All of us made it back OK. We had not predicted that something like that would happen and we were euphoric that day. We had already started feeling more powerful the night before as people started going out onto the streets, we started breathing deeper. From the beginning it seemed to us that we had to participate because something interesting was happening at the level of the people. We couldn't sit still, we came here, we met up, we discussed, we called each other on the phone. We spent all our time in our movement spaces, nobody stayed at home. There were constant assemblies, large and small, and the conversation ranged from the looting to what was happening in Plaza de Mayo, from the food that the government was sending and the benefit packages we were renewing. We talked about a mix of things, but you couldn't help but note the euphoria in the comrades. Especially since we were coming off a moment of great anxiety and we knew that Congress was getting ready to vote on a budget plan that included major austerity measures. We had even been saying to friends that if the Argentine people didn't play their card soon, we were going to lose. We saw that the situation was very complicated with Cavallo's advance and his economic policies, the new measures, the repression. We were anxious about that and we thought that it was very unlikely that there would be a reaction like this that would put an end to the economic model that was destroying us. So, it was an explosion of adrenaline, of wanting to participate because we knew that was the way to get rid of Cavallo.

But we also had the sensation that we were "one." When we reached the Plaza, we were scared, things were intense and a lot of young people had come with us and we were responsible for them. There were rumors of deaths, but we knew that we were participating in something historic. You could feel the solidarity, we were no longer *piqueterxs*, we were no longer middle: everyone felt that sensation of being "one." People threw down water for us to drink from their balconies, threw water on us when there was a lot of gas, they threw hot oil on the cops. Comrades would come running from one direction and say "don't go that way, the cops are there." There was a very strong sense of unity, without flags, we were one. That is, the flags were not needed. I think that all of us who were there shared the same objective – stop this shit economy – and we also shared great hope for what that meant. Something was ending, and therefore hope in something new was reborn, at least in that moment that was experienced that way, with a great deal of intensity. It was with the announcement that De La Rúa was renouncing the presidency that we decided to go back to our neighborhood because we had received phone calls that several comrades had been detained. We were very worried about what would happen here in the neighborhood, because we had only partially carried out our action plan. So, we decided to come back and see how things were going.

We spent some time analyzing the players on the different stages: who was present and made an effort on the side of the people, and who allied with the other side, with the government. We saw that many of those who up until that moment had supposedly supported the popular side, operated on the side of the government. We know that they were reserved that day, and not because they were naïve. Thus, we saw that certain things within the popular field were starting to be defined, at least among the organized sectors in struggle.

It also opened an important discussion about the issue of the middle class and the *cacerolazos*. We asked ourselves: where is this going, who is leading it, how is it coordinated? At first, we really did not understand how all of this was organized; and later, as things were going on, we realized that it was a combination of many spontaneous things. Later, the assemblies, the debates, started, but at the beginning it was all very spontaneous. It is very powerful, at least for us. In the MTD, this sparked reflections and debates. Nothing is the same after the December 20. History has been changed, that's how we experience it.

We asked ourselves many things. For example, the assemblies were saying "they all must go," some political parties and organizations started saying that it was time to overthrow the government. We differentiate ourselves a little from this, we understand that we have to go at our own pace. We have been attending several assemblies, going to Parque Centenario, and participating more seriously in the assembly in Avellaneda. We have marched with them, blocked roads together, but we don't go with flags. They know that we are from the MTD, that we are *piqueterxs*, but we understand that no one can put a flag, a label, on this struggle. We think that the struggle needs to be unified, but nobody can homogenize it. We all have to take the streets together, attack power together, but nobody owns this struggle. We contribute what we can to this this struggle and we do not think, as some comrades do, that since we *piqueterxs* started the struggle, we should be privileged in it.

It is not difficult to realize that there is something that did not that December, but rather continues. It is starting to take on a more defined expression that shows that there is an attempt to create something new. Starting with putting an end to the representation practiced by those politicians, the seeds of what we want this society to be are being sown: a society without a chamber of deputies, without senators, and instead with an assembly that makes decisions without representation and its whole circus. We also feel a bit of disappointment when we see that party flags are starting to fly again, and we have been noting that the assemblies are also invaded by undercover "militants" – party activists who do not declare themselves as such, who attempt to impose their party line.

Today there is a lot of debate around politics. In our case, the expectations come more from outside and not from within the movement. In regards to the national political gatherings of certain *piqueterx* groups and leftist parties, some comrades called us to ask if we were going to attend, what we were going to do. In the Aníbal Verón Coordinator, we also discussed whether or not we should participate, and only a small number of people argued that we had to go and that it was necessary to arrive in a super large column to show everyone that we are the biggest group. But the majority of us argued that no, we are in another time frame of construction. Like MTD Solano, we think that the struggle is going to be long, we think that the repression will get worse, and we don't think that there will be revolutionary change in favor of the people. Obviously, it is very interesting that the struggle is generalizing and undoubtedly, one has to be there and not just look at it from the outside, but we think that it is a longer process than what some people expect today, at least in the imaginary that is circulating. We have to go slower, and not get stuck in a corner, because there is still a long way to go. We have to consolidate what we are building. It would be a shame to lose the ability to articulate and consolidate worthwhile things with organizations such as the APENOC, MOCASE,[22] and, outside of Argentina, with the MST in Brazil, the experiences of farmers in Paraguay, in other words, with so many organizations with other forms of movement building. It would be a mistake to not take the opportunity to materialize all of that, to jump into "the other," that we think will be cut off. For us, that would be a loss, a step back on the terrain of popular struggles.

---

22   Movimiento Campesino de Santiago de Estero, the Campesino Movement of Santiago de Estero (a province in northwest Argentina), affiliated with Via Campesina. For more information, see the booklet *Situaciones 3. Conversations with MOCASE; De Mano en Mano,* Buenos Aires, September 2001.

This issue of radicalization is also on everyone's minds, in fact, some comrades are questioning the action plan. We have to go out, on the defensive, if you will, because there is a change in government policy in regards to popular organizations and their autonomy. There is a direct attack, that is proposed through the crisis committees and the municipal government: a new return to the traditional model of control is hidden in the proposal for transparency, democracy, and justice; a plan to not allow organizations that are not within the state apparatus to develop. However, we have never doubted that we had to maintain a firm position to defend our autonomy and everything that we were able to achieve, in one way or the other, over the last year. But we see that the issue of the vanguard is appearing in other organizations. They think the we are in a moment of political orphanage, in which the people cannot find a channel for their discontent, and therefore it is the responsibility of the revolutionaries to say where things should go and to mark the path. We don't share this view. Furthermore, when we hear "they all must go," we also include the leftist parties, and it seems that they don't recognize that. But they are part of the old, and they could end up destroying this experience. We trust that all of these people who are sick and tired of the same old thing will have the capacity to not mess up this experience that is germinating: in assemblies, in direct democracy, in the autonomy from all union and political representation. So, when we say "they all must go," we want political parties to step aside, and take all their outdated ways of understanding the process of struggle with them. It infuriates us, even when comrades who we know are honest, committed militants cannot understand and see beyond their schemas, and that could ruin this process. We hope that this develops and matures, beyond the crisis that we know is coming.

But we are very happy to see this initiative, this genuine search for democracy without representation, without any of the old ways. The discussion is heading in that direction. For us, it was never about "grassroots work" versus "political work": it is not a matter of maturing the conditions of the unemployed so that, at some other moment, they can take up politics. We don't make that distinction, but many comrades do and they argue: "so far we have been fighting for this, but now it is time for politics." We don't share this vision; in fact, we are going to continue strengthening our everyday work, with its gray areas, that is very heroic, although many comrades think that it is more heroic to be at the head of the vanguard, breaking everything. We are not going to give up on this everyday construction: that is our decision.

What we need is to go deeper. Since December, we have only had a few moments of calm; we need to be able to reflect, and not only in Solano, but also with other comrades. There is a risk that "reality" will devour us; we are very practical, but we run the risk of superficiality. We have to find the times and spaces for deeper reflection, because sometimes things get out of place, there are things in the air and they have an effect on us, things that are happening in society.

Now we are presented with a new situation, because the Partido Justicialista is reconstructing its apparatus, in the form of a network, by recuperating strong economic power. One of the challenges we face is consolidating ourselves here, because we know that now the struggle will be face-to-face. They are going to put their whole apparatus to work and that has certain repercussions for us: from repression to competition. That is how they understand it, because, as we see it, our fight is not for power, but rather we are defending our work. Nonetheless, they do all of this to counteract autonomous organizations.

So, for us, that is one of the challenges, we have talked about this a lot together. We still have a long way to go, there is a lot to learn, and we are preparing for the worst. Hopefully the worst will not come, but it would be terrible for it to catch you by surprise and not be prepared for the attacks, which sometimes come in the form of rumors or defamation, or sometimes they directly send their men to break up your assembly. These are the challenges: to reinforce the areas of popular education, the neighborhood work, unity with neighborhood residents outside the movement. In that sense, we are following the path laid by the comrades of Mosconi of trying to rebuild the fabric of the community, in the service of the common good, the environment, health, children, and other unresolved problems in the neighborhood.

What autonomous organizations have in their favor is that the system that this government represents cannot provide solutions to the fundamental problems, such as unemployment, health care, and education. The creates a frame of conflict that, in some ways, cannot be hegemonized by the work of the *punteros*, because the *punteros* can give out one hundred benefits packages, but there will be a hundred thousand more people waiting. I'm not trying to say that the worse, the better, but I remember in 1996 or 1997 when, faced with the smallest demand, Duhalde would provide an immediate response. And they can no longer do that, they can't respond to everything anymore. So, they can attack us but it is going to be difficult to destroy us. Sometimes we say that they will destroy us when this society changes, because if they want to destroy us, they will have to build a better society.

About the 26th of June[23]

I

At the end of June, the *piqueterx* mobilizations returned to the streets. On June 26, to be precise, several groups prepared an action plan, with demonstrations and roadblocks in the whole urban periphery of Buenos Aires. The government decided to publicly prohibit blockades on the bridges that connect the province of Buenos Aires to the Capital. These bridges have a long history: whenever the multitudes are activated, these bridges are their central path into the city. Not even the rising tensions in the days before the protests could have foretold the police attack that was unleashed on that day. Hundreds of people were injured and – legally and illegally – detained; a police chief actually shot two comrades from the *piqueterx* movement. The police have so much immunity that they murdered them in front of witnesses, journalists, and even photographers: everything was perfectly recorded.

Everything, except the fact that the chief and his officers were just a small part of a *greater* problem, escapes us. While the police are obviously responsible for what happened, and it is also necessary to expand the circle of guilt to include many *others*, limiting the analysis of what happened to determining who is responsible for the murders does not come close to explaining what happened. In effect, June 26 – like December 19 and 20 – is another meaningful date, a new marker on the social body that reveals fundamental dimensions of the composition of the present, aspects that still have not been fully understood, but must be addressed.

It is because the mechanisms that were activated that morning, and that surely

---

23 This text introduces the third part of the book, composed of the work that was carried out between July and October of 2002. It was elaborated on the bases of the declaration of the Colectivo Situaciones after the massacre on June 26 on the Pueyrredón Bridge where two militants from the Aníbal Verón Unemployed Workers' Organization, Darío Santillán and Maximilliano Kosteki, were killed.

were designed to produce an ever-greater advance in the repressive forces, seem to have repeated the same parabola as the events of December. As you can remember, on June 19 the national government declared the *state of siege* throughout the country. It claimed – just listen to the pathetic discourse of the then President of the nation to see this – "to protect the population" from violent acts (robberies and looting) carried out by the new specters of neoliberalism: "the excluded." But everything dissolved when the state of siege was immediately and treacherously ignored by the very population that they supposedly wanted to protect. We all know how events unfolded.

Nonetheless, something symptomatic can be seen on those dates.

It is not about, as can be imagined at first glance, the repressive bankruptcy of the state and nothing more: there are deaths from both dates to prove it. But there is what can be conceived as the *failure* of the Argentinean State to *legitimize* – and therefore generalize as an unnoticed legal policy – these repressive acts. We are not, we insist, confronted with an absolute failure, but rather a *relative* one; but it does have a profound significance that provides us with possibilities for thinking.

II

According to Foucault, sovereign power had the privilege to *"make die or let live."* The death penalty and calling citizens to war speaks to us of this ability, which characterizes a historic form of power based on the appropriation of things, time, and in the last instance, life. Every time that the sovereign kills, nonetheless, they have to explain their reasons in a way that is not a mere whim, but rather an act carried out in the name of the collective *body* that they are supposed to represent.

This "sovereign power" has longed ceased to be the principal dynamic of the powers that *produce* (and at the same time *repress*) the *social body*. Thus, what we know as "society" (modern, bourgeoisie) is a body that was produced, over the course of the last three centuries, by a complex constellation of dispositifs of power that Foucault referred to as disciplinary (the family, the school, the factory, institutions of seclusion such as asylums and prisons, and the police). It is this *disciplinary society* that, during our times, has started to come under attack: the *crisis* of public institutions and institutions of confinement attack it head on. The mechanisms of the "production of society" seem to be fraying and, in their place, there is only room for the logic installed by virtual market forces. Are we facing a "crisis of domination" or "the start of a new form of domination"? These seem to be the *political* questions of the time.

Foucault did not say much in this regard. At most a few pages and it is not totally clear to us how they help us think about the present. Foucault referred – in his last pages – to the emergence of a *biopower*. Biopower produces a collective body, but it no longer the social – political – body, but a *biological* power of the "population" – *bio-politics*. Its principal function is no longer to kill, but to invade life. This biopower takes responsibility for the *governability* of the life of human populations – of the mechanisms and aptitudes belonging to the species. This bio-political state takes charge of the care, production, and ordering of the life of the population and its privilege adopts a new nature: *to make live or let die.*

Nonetheless, in biopolitical conditions, the state does not disappear or abandon its old sovereign capacities. It also kills. And, as in the case of the old sovereign power, it must take care to not do so without adequate justifications.

The question seems to be, then, the following: *How does the state kill* in biopolitical conditions? How does it decide whose life is worth protecting and who will the *sacrificed*?

This is not a neutral question, since it seems to push us to recognize what appears to be a "technical" difference between the death *produced* by biopolitical mechanisms – the growing power of "letting die" – and the privilege of the sovereign, *to kill.*

III

But things cannot be so easily separated: the state kills based on a prior biopolitical selection: it kills, but not just anyone: it chooses – especially – from among those *devalued* lives that it is always (already) *letting die.* We know that it is not the same to kill the included (*privileged life that power "makes live"*) as the excluded (*life that power "lets die"*). A "robber" is not killed in the same was as an "investor" (nor is it the same between a "local investor" and a "banker"). People are not killed in the same way in the *center* and the *periphery*. In fact, *people are killed all the time in the periphery.*

The *decision* (or the mere *possibility*) to kill, therefore, involves a twofold operation: the selection of a population that is presented as a threat to the "protected" (the authentic meaning of the "included") and later, carrying out murder under some sort of juridical (police) cover.

The first operation implies the *peripheralization* of the territory and the *criminalization* of those bodies, ultimately, the *devaluing* of those lives. The second operation, on the other hand, requires taking into account issues related to the technique of killing, the economy of repression, and its legal forms.

Therefore, the deaths that occurred on December 20 and those that took place on June 26 share the same scandalous character – for power – now that both confirm a *failure*, an *error* that became clear in the *sovereign operation*. The *error* seemed to be *comprehensive* and attacks the truthfulness of the "official" versions. No one believes that they tried to "protect" the ("included") population from "looters," in the first place, and from "piqueterxs," second (and it is not a matter of denying the existence of those who feel "insecure" because of the "looting" and the "roadblocks." It is clear that there are people who feel that way, and probably more than we would like to believe).

Effectively, there are different versions of the story in both cases: in December, it was a matter of the poor who were "controlled" by Peronist clientelist networks; in the second, of "piqueterxs" killing "piqueterxs" (versions that, it is worth remembering, were initially shared across a wide range of "communication" channels, including "progressives" who were willing to circulate and support those stories).

But the failure of the operation goes beyond the inability to present truthful "motives" for the specific punitive actions. There is a deeper issue, it is about the state's inability to carry out its *biopolitical regulating functions*, that is, to "take responsibility for life" and "take care of the population." That *failure*, it seems, has to do with the very heart of the foundations of the state's existence and affects its credentials as "defender of life" in the face of "biological" threats (racial, class-based, etc.) that are constantly activated as useful threats for the formation of the biopolitical body.

IV

The events of June 26 seem to shed light on the existence of a larger antagonism: that which speaks to us of the emergence of a counter-power, of a project for a "parallel society" that has been developed in recent years and has deepened – and been rendered visible – since December 2001. Nonetheless, it is not a matter of going back to the situation of the 1970s, nor to the military dictatorship, but rather a singular opening that demands to be addressed in all its contemporaneity.

On one side, there is the *project* of constructing a state capable of regulating, reinforcing, and multiplying sovereign and biopolitical powers. The *nation state* as we have known it, almost no longer exists and was substituted by a form of complex regulation, which includes mafia-like webs, with their armed groups (both "official" and paramilitary), and direct forms of articulation with global capital. It is difficult to predict what this new *domination pact* will look like (or even if that pact with be effectively possible and lasting). In any case, those possibilities concern us when what is at stake, from this perspective, is the possibility of sustaining and the intensifying the savage recolonization that is underway.[24]

In this context, state violence is increasingly traversed by the logic of "armed gangs," some of which act on the basis of degrees of institutional consistency (federal and provincial police, gendarmerie, the national guard, etc.), while others function directly as para-police groups and gangs for security agencies – which have become true private armies – at the direct service of companies and/or fractions of political power. And it is often impossible to make clear distinctions between these forms of operating.

Ultimately, the dictatorship has ended. The violence of power is no longer demonstrated in the same way as it was twenty-five or thirty years ago. This does not mean, of course, that these modes of violence have disappeared or that, as we often see, they do not operate with the same characters and procedures. But it does mean that those procedures and characters no longer need a classical coup d'état to increase the violence against popular initiatives, but rather that these procedures – and many others – become compatible with new forms of political, economic, and institutional articulation.

On the other side are the constituent forces of counter-power, which move through the fraying social body in a transversal way, in neighborhoods, neighborhood assemblies, schools, universities, hospitals, worker-managed recuperated factories, and highways all across Argentina. These are "points of *potencia*" that take responsibility for "life," but no longer based on the postulates of biopower, but rather its opposites: "life" is not something to "care for," to "govern," something merely biological to "protect," but rather a *productive force to multiply,* to de-biologicize, as a *source of creation* and not as an "object to care for" (and control). It is clear that the *piqueterx* experiences find their meaning within this new social landscape.

As such, the repression on June 26 cannot be understood outside of these circumstances.

V

These were some of the concerns that motivated us to revitalize and reorient the workshop with MTD Solano. The shared intuition of what had happened in June opened new challenges and the desire to take them on, to understand them, deciding that since mid-July, week after week, we will generate the necessary time to get

---

24 Savage recolonization that, like the EZLN says, is in the origin of the so called "forth world war" that is nothing other than the clash between new colonizing powers and resistance against them.

to the bottom of these problems. This is an accomplishment in and of itself, it we take into account the enormous difficulty involved in creating spaces for thought when our subjectivities are filled by an immeasurable whirlpool of sadness, rage, and impotence for the loss of dear comrades and the intimate experience of the fragility of our lives and our projects.

This intensity lies under each one of the interventions that compose the central text of the third part of this book and are the result of an edited transcription of the different workshop meetings.

The starting point for these meetings was a text called "Twelve hypotheses on counter-power." We shared this text with the comrades from MTD Solano and used it to kick off discussions in the workshop.

Twelve Hypotheses about Counter-power

1. **A situational perspective allows us to examine the concrete "possibilities" that the acceleration of time impedes us from discovering. "Urgency" as a demand of the conjuncture and the mass media, in other words, of the world of representation, tends to submerge us in sadness. It is not a matter of isolating ourselves, but rather addressing the issues of the conjuncture based on a concrete situation, returning again and again to the concrete possibilities made possible or impossible by the situation.**

In earlier meetings we talked about the difference between *dispersion* and *multiplicity*. Dispersion leads to isolation, it impoverishes. But the alternative to dispersion is not necessarily centralization or bureaucratization.

There is no reason for experiences that think based on their own situation to become isolated. To the contrary, situational thinking is nothing more than the act of reconnecting with our own capacities and circumstances: it means thinking based on the concrete and with the objective of the concrete.

The *situational* and the *local* are not the same thing. The local is the territorial delimitation of the global. Therefore, the local is a portion of the global. The local is as abstract as the global. The situational, on the other hand, is the fact that, based on our experience, we can elaborate a point of view that is practical, but also theoretical, about the issues that concern us.

It is not a question, then, of "moving away" from reality. To the contrary, the experience of self-affirmation is characterized by clinging to the situation. Far from dispersion and isolation, this type of experience always opens new possibilities for practice and thought. It shows us something fundamental: *there are always more options than those that conjuncture presents to us as the only possibilities. And that is precisely the importance of thinking: discovering the possibilities that exist in the concrete situation.*

2. **The logic of confrontation, as an exaltation of the moment of battle, of violence as a wager on the offensive, lies in opposition to situational self-affir-**

mation. It is a resource for power more than for *potencia*. It tends to believe that the conjuncture itself is a unique situation and subordinates everything to the struggle for power in that scenario. It also tends toward centralization.

Another major problem of the "logic of confrontation" is that it tends to understand struggle according to a mirror logic: it loses the fundamental difference been "one and the other," it ignores all asymmetry. The violence of power that seeks to appropriate the other's *potencia* is not the same as the counter-power that seeks to protect forms of life that are alternatives to those that capital produces.

As such, violence is never excluded as a possibility. Rather, in the experiences of counter-power, violence is present in multiple forms: legal and illegal repression, the violence of the market, etc.

But additionally, violence is a resource of *potencia*. The roadblock, self-defense, and specific offensives, are all political forms of violence of those from below. This is obvious. Violence cannot be judged based on a moral value. But, at the same time, the fact that violence "comes from below" does not necessarily indicate that it is tied to the emergence of an alternative sociability: just because it is comprehensible and more legitimate, does not make it, in itself, capable of *producing* an alternative sociability.

Two key aspects appear as possibilities for thinking about the forms of a violence that does not separate itself from or turn its back on the emergence of an alternative sociability: first, that it be based on an authentically defensive conception. That is not to say that it does not have its own initiative. It is not a law about how to act. It simply refers to the fact that acts of self-defense are driven by popular resources, not power, and especially that those actions are not oriented around acquiring-obtaining power, but rather the defense of an emergent sociability and the *potencia* of those experiences. Second, multiplicity as a form that is *different* from dispersion and centralization, in accordance with the reality of the experiences of counter-power and as a resource against isolation in a specialized "apparatus."

The offensive, as a conception of violence, is a weapon of the enemy, of central power, of the "powerful" in general (understanding the powerful to be those who control another's *potencia*). Offensive violence is conquering, colonial, and imperialist. That is why war is the terrain of power. Power siwants to drive its enemies there. Yet, more than a few times, the people feel they can attack power. Nonetheless, the people do not choose the wars. The people shoulder the majority of the deaths. Popular war is not desirable. It should only be taken on when imposed, and therefore, a final hypothesis is that it is totally undesirable.

Thus, when open confrontation as a privileged space for defining political struggle tends to become the dominant logic, it opens the door to the naked power of death. That logic is not only attractive for armies and guerrilla struggles, but also for political parties, intellectuals, and social movements: *the logic of confrontations is part of the dominant version of politics as the "struggle for power."* In effect, if politics is the confrontation between two sides fighting over central power, offensive war is the only strategy for both contestants, competing to the death, equating them to an unimaginable point. As such, it has no relation to the defensive war of the people for independence and against colonialism and imperialism that we have seen in the twentieth century.

For experiences of counter-power, violence is an unavoidable element from the moment that it becomes present through all types of injustices and forms of repression, but also as its own resource. But there is no reason to equate it with the violence of power. Its differences come from being multiple (not centralized) in the multiple (one resource among others), and an inevitably defensive conception. Therefore, the true choice is not between violence and non-violence, but between self-affirmation and the logic of confrontation.

3. **Violence is present and is also a situational resource. If it is made unilateral, it becomes logic of confrontation. But if the opposite occurs, it can become the active defense of a newly produced sociability.**

Violence is a situational resource, thus there is absolutely no reason to mechanically identify *violence* with the *logic of confrontation.* History is full of examples of intelligent and legitimate violence. To condemn violence in general is to fall into an abstract, pre-political, ahistorical way of thinking. Violence is present and we have to take it on, not deny it.

It is therefore essential, in this respect, to separate confrontation as one of multiple possibilities in a situation from the logic of confrontation that tends to monopolize everything to increasingly become the only route possible. Our recent history shows us the risks of militarism and other forms of polarization that tend to construct counter-power as a mirror of power, dividing everything in two, and founding "symmetries" between both forces.

Violence as a resource of the multitude has no reason to reproduce this mirror logic. To the contrary, the violence of the masses, when it seeks to affirm itself in its *potencia*, is defensive, and is founded on the asymmetry of forces, legitimacy, and resources.

On the other hand, violence as one resource among many can very well co-exist with other resources of the situation, preventing the confrontation from "taking power" over the other possibilities that always exist.

That said, the core of a defensive conception consists of the fact that the legitimacy and efficacy of any type of violence that does not want to become the mirror of power, lies in its defensive character itself, on the one hand; and, on the other, in that "what it defends is defensive": that is, alternative forms of life. In the last instance, the debate around violence rests on the existence of those forms. In this respect, the examples of the MST in Brazil and the Indigenous communities in Chiapas and their relationship with the EZLN are illustrative.

4. **In the *piquete*, three different, parallel and complementary, forms of relation with the state take place at the same time: 1) the state represses; 2) the state ignores the demands and conditions of the neighborhood; 3) the state funds benefit packages and projects. Insofar as the objective of the roadblock is to obtain benefit packages and funding for social projects, violence, as a resource, is inevitable. Thus, there is a real risk of getting trapped in a logic of confrontation, proposed and promoted by the government (but not only by the government). And therefore, it is fundamental to build, starting from that reality, increasingly autonomous experiences, capable of preparing for the reduction in subsidies, on the one hand, and, on the other, taking the resource of war away from power, so that the autonomous *piqueterx* organizations do not get dragged down that path.**

We know that there is not one *piqueterx* movement. There are many. Nonetheless, they all share the roadblock. It is true that each one carries out roadblocks in their own way (completely or partially shutting down the road, wearing masks or not, etc.). However, there is still something they have in common: making demands on the state (whether the municipal, provincial, or national government) for benefit packages and social projects, and using the roadblock as a weapon to apply pressure.

We discussed this issue last year. At that time, we identified three tendencies in the *piqueterx* movement: two that understand themselves based on *globality* and the *conjuncture* (which include both the self-defined "revolutionaries" and those who fight for inclusion in the system through "reformism"). Each has different strategies but they share a way of conceiving politics: as a form of thought and practice based on the conjuncture. In contrast, the MTD Solano was developing another possibility in the affirmation of situational thought and acting.

After December 19 and 20, the movements re-accommodated themselves to the conjuncture. Some disappeared and others wanted to be the vanguard. In one of the workshop meetings, we discussed the importance of rejecting the illusion of a political vacuum. On that occasion, it was said that the priority was to expand our grassroots work and produce our own times and spaces, in which to have a sovereignty that would allow us to think about everything, including the conjuncture.

It is worth repeating that, among so many differences, there is one thing that all the movements share: the roadblock. As a moment of making demands on the state, it becomes an inevitable site of confrontation. The state only recognizes those whom it subordinates or those who confront it. The MTD's choice, therefore, means an inevitable level of violence linked to making demands on an increasingly devastated state.

Let's look at this more closely: in the roadblock, three different, parallel, and complementary, forms of relation with the state take place: confrontation, negotiation, and indifference. It is a difficult, contradictory, paradoxical situation, but there is no other choice but to take it on. And the movement's capacity, in large part, rests on knowing how to combining these three realities. The first conclusion we can draw is that *while it is necessary to make demands on the state, all the variants are present in variable proportions. And therefore, confrontation is inevitable.*

It is for this reason that it is of vital importance to consolidate alternative forms of reproducing the movement's existence that no longer rely on the benefit packages as the only and central resource.

5. **The perspective of experiences that sustain themselves in their own capacity, in their *potencia* and project this energy, find their force in the process of self-affirmation. The keys for their development are located in their capacity to remove themselves from the times and demands of the conjuncture and representation in order to produce their own time. For counter-power, politics is, primarily, the capacity to produce that temporality, that autonomy.**

Autonomy, independence, and self-affirmation are not obvious and are not achieved once and for all. They are not easy to obtain or easy to sustain once achieved. It is a *permanent task.*

The fact that autonomy cannot be complete, at least not for now, opens different possibilities.

This can lead to a supposed realism that tells us that "politics" of negotiation, alliances, the electoral realm, is the only thing that is left to us to control, once and for all, the state itself. Another position says "let's take advantage of the state," "as we confront it, we will accumulate force" to the point of "taking the state itself." Both positions end up being the same, because they constitute two different strategies based on the same underlying belief: change comes from controlling the national state, and that politics is astuteness and the struggle for power.

But there is another possibility: the politics of self-affirmation. However, this is not easy, because it always depends on two principles that are difficult to achieve and, especially, difficult to develop once they are achieved. First, a greater capacity to establish our own times, issues, resources, spaces, and initiatives. These capacities are, already, difficult to find in politics, because they depend on a position that does not seek resources for war, but rather an option for life, everyday reproduction, daily rebellion, and the need to avoid the traps of power. And, second, there is no autonomy without interdependence: it is impossible to obtain one's own space, time, thought, and resources without developing a web of counter-power capable of comprehensibly reproducing the movement.

A new conclusion that can be drawn is that the autonomy of potencia involves a self-affirmation that founds a new sovereignty (spatial and temporal) that is capable of withdrawing itself from the norms of capital. But, in order to do so, potencia must expand, find and connect with other experiences, weaving together autonomous reproductive circuits.

To move forward along this path, three observations are vitally important: 1) the need to deal with the state does not mean it is impossible to develop, in a parallel manner, autonomous options; 2) self-affirmation tends to be based on a practical hypothesis of the autonomous reproduction of the experience (and its projection); and 3) it is important to produce, in parallel, a political analysis of counter-power that allows for understanding the phenomena of the conjuncture with the fundamental objective of producing, sustaining, and protecting the experiences of counter-power.

6. **The state has transformed. It is degrading. It has been held hostage by neo-liberal politics, by the acceleration of the global flows of capital (so-called globalization), and it has been appropriated by true mafias. A new social formation is emerging in Argentina: social fragmentation, mass impover-ishment, and the destruction of the old productive structure. The *piqueterxs* recognize this transformation.**

    What does this novelty mean for the thought that emerges from experi-ences of counter-power? Two things seem clear: 1) the current state is no longer the (not so) old nation-state, with its effective capacities of integra-tion, even if they were always limited; and 2) there are currently important resources of domination that unfold, to a relative degree, outside of the neoliberal-mafioso-state.

This current state is being dismembered. On one side, it was emptied out by neoliberal policies. On the other side, according to those who have much more information than we do, the mafias have taken over state apparatuses. Finally, there are more than enough testimonies showing that it is no longer functional in areas that used to be its fundamental tasks. It is not that the state has disappeared, nor is it on the road to extinction. But yes, it has changed. It is not that it is now weaker or stronger, but simply that some of its roles and priorities have changed, as well as the ways that it carries them out.

On the one hand, the lack of attention to basic services, such as health care and public education, pensions, and, in general terms, essential services for the lives of much of the population, is clear. On the other hand, the state has given up even on some of the tasks that have been fundamental tasks of the capitalist state. At the moment, *there is no monopoly on legally circulating currency*. Not only for the bonds produced by the national and provincial governments, that maintain a certain state legality, but because of the circulation of "credits" in all the barter networks. In Quilmes, for example, there was a plan to pay taxes with credits from the Global Barter Network. Another powerful example is the defense of private property: during the looting in December, the large transnational supermarkets directly contracted personnel from the police or gendarmerie to repress would-be looters, while the small and medium sized grocery strokes were defended at gunpoint by their own owners. We can list example after example: police gangs that become autonomous from legal and political power, mafia warfare, private security agencies, para-police groups, massive corruption at all levels, etc.

These examples reveal that the national state is no longer, currently (at least in Argentina), the only and sufficient resource of domination. It is true that it never was completely, but now, more so than other times, it would be an illusion to believe that domination is mostly controlled by the state apparatus. On the one hand, there are the market resources: publicity, media, production of images of happiness and fulfillment, desire for consumption, the determination of new forms of inclusion and exclusion, etc. On the other hand, there are new forms of control that are no longer organized by the state apparatus, although they have its relative authorization (for example, within supermarkets or factories), and finally, the para-militarization, the mafia, that has taken over the state apparatus, but that directly articulates with the large corporations (private security agencies and the illegal direct sale of services of state resources).

In this context, one thing seems certain: *the loss of the state's regulatory capacity demonstrates the inexistence of the old national state that sought to integrate the population, even with all its limitations.* This situation raises new challenges both for those who organize domination and for counter-power.

Capital faces the challenge of constructing the minimum forms of state regulation. This can mean attempting to build a neoliberal state that is able to enforce the law, that is, recomposing, in new terms, a political authority founded on its technical capacity to develop business in the country; or, to the contrary, directly associating itself with, as it has up until now, the mafia state, which constitute nuclei of regulation outside of the state, without reversing the decomposition and corruption of the state apparatus.

These possibilities should take into account that the mafia state exists and, as such, constitutes a powerful point of departure for any analysis or project on the level of the organization of domination (designated by the need of capital valorization), therefore any result will be intermediary between these possibilities. These options are also crossed by other fundamental movements of the global, continental, and national conjuncture that we have not even mentioned yet, but that reveal a greater level of complexity and that have a direct relationship with the imperialist forces that want Argentina to join the FTAA.

We insist on what seems to be of the most importance to us now: 1) *the end of the national state as we know it; 2) a reorganization of domination that involves a combination of old resources along with new modalities.*

7. **Capital needs to recompose its dominion and it still does not seem to have a single strategy or a clear way of doing so. The national conjuncture is characterized by this fundamental fact. It is not a matter of a power vacuum, but a more complex process. The question is what type of capitalism is possible in the current context determined as much by political and institutional degradation as by the presence of extended networks of counter-power.**

It often seems as though political reality is presented in two ways: what appears when we think of it immediately, as a reflex, and what is revealed when we think about it more deeply.

Reflex thinking tends to reproduce what the media and politicians say. We think about our reality as if what has already happened in the past will necessarily be repeated, as if history operated according to cyclical time. So, for example, the Triple A are in the government, and today's guerrillas are the ones resisting and today, 2002, is going to be something like 1975.[25] Then, all is left is to wait for a

---

25 The "Triple A" refers to the Argentine Anticommunist Alliance, a far-right death squad that operated between 1973-1976, targeting any leftist opponents of the government, and which has been found responsible for crimes against humanity. 1975 was a year marked by intense political violence, from the Triple A and other right-wing groups, as well as left-wing guerrilla movements, which ultimately lead to a coup, in which a military dictatorship came to power. – Trans.

victorious insurrection that avoids the final death, or a repressive dictatorship that repeats history.

Only when we think more seriously, in other words, with our own minds, based on what we experience in our own circumstances, can we see that neither the media nor the politicians, nor the consecrated intellectuals truly think, rather they "know things" (honestly or dishonestly, depending on the case). But thought must be produced anew each time, each one of us, in our situation.

Doing so, we discover that history does not repeat itself and while there are clear continuities, they tend to develop new meanings, even if they seem very subtle and minor at first glance.

It is in this sense that we have to ask ourselves again whether the current conjuncture is just another repetition of the many things we have already seen or if, in its singularity, it is showing us something that is worth the effort to understand.

On the one hand, the current conjuncture is illuminated when it is perceived based on transformations, in the heat of the destitution of the national state, as we analyzed in the previous point.

On the other hand, the current crisis has managed to render visible the development of experiences of counter-power and accelerated their growth.

In this context, the needs of power include: 1) producing opportunities for re-initiating a process of capitalist accumulation, and to do so, it requires, 2) recomposing forms of regulation, which means minimally recomposing certain state functions (political power, legitimacy, including for repression, etc.) and 3) resolving its co-existence (in more or less repressive terms) with the networks of counter-power.

Here we are not trying to develop a meticulous panorama of the international or national conjuncture (although it is clear that these are problems of the utmost importance, particularly the explosion of the crisis across Latin America), nor of the struggle that is currently developing within the dominant class bloc, nor party politics superstructure game. No, it is primarily about insisting that is worth taking this context into account in order to develop consistent hypotheses within the experiences of counter-power.

Let's return to the issue of the mafia-state. It is not just a state form. It is also a form of social regulation that extends throughout the very bases of society. Its dynamic spreads a de-institutionalized violence founded on internal struggles (whether political, business, or police struggles, all of which are articulated and submerged in the same conspiratorial, hidden, mode). Its current articulation with global capital does not mean an expansion of socio-economic inclusion, but rather brings the population together in complete degradation.

A hypothetical efficient administrative state, articulated with a recomposition of capital investment (eventually, and in the best of cases, based on a massive proletarianization of the middle classes) would have to coexist with this panorama and articulate with this mafia state.

Even in that case, which seems to be the panacea of "Argentinean progressivism," the use of violence would continue. Repressive violence would be more targeted, but not necessarily less generalized. In all cases, repression would tend to be applied against the obstacles that "the excluded, the radicals" exert on new business, to the circuits of capital valorization. It is clear that the roadblock, therefore, lies in the center of all repressive hypotheses.

If what we have said so far is not simply delirious (and we can make no promises that it is not), we can draw one more conclusion: the coexistence of the power of capital with counter-power, not only guarantees physical repressions in the future. That is only one aspect, which, furthermore, is already seen in the present. There is also the possibility of "compromise."

If capitalism's subsistence involves producing business, the maturity of experiences of counter-power (as such) would involve both coexisting with repression (in whatever form it appears) and with co-optation, which is no longer, as it used to be, generalized integration led by the state (as it was under Peronism from 1946 to 1952), but rather more degraded forms of gift-giving, clientelism, proletarianization in hyper-precarious conditions, etc.

If, as we have supposed, the state (trapped as it is in the networks of capital) lacks the ability to substantially expand social inclusion on its own, we find ourselves confronted with a face-to-face relationship between, on one side, capital (and its mafia-state articulation), its repressive capacities, and co-optation and, on the other side, counter-power and its project to create autonomy. And there is no truly effective mediation between both forces. Thus, *compromise* (co-optation, precarious inclusion) and *repression* (especially of those who block the circuits of capital valorization, but also due to internal mafias) are two variants that, either combined or not, will become present as long as coexistence between the power of capital and counter-power continues.

8. **In effect, class struggle – in the current circumstances – takes off around a power that seeks to and needs to appropriate and control natural, cultural, and vital processes (capital) and the forces of resistance, which will manage to take up the challenge of producing another sociability if they are capable of generating a new way of producing life: external to, opposed to, and more powerful than the regime of capital. There are very rich experiences in this respect across Latin America.**

In effect, we think that class struggle revolves around the fundamental fact that capital tends to dominate the environment, human life, and cultural wealth in an increasingly direct way. It is clear across Latin America how community's struggles to control their own conditions of reproduction enter into direct contradiction with the needs of capital accumulation.

Everything that is subordinated to capital is brutally exploited. Capitalism, more than ever, produces life for death. Its own mode of accumulation structurally generates exclusion. The moment of greatest productivity in the history of humankind is also that of the most misery.

On the other hand, the strength of struggles increasingly lies in their tendencies to *become autonomous from capital's command.* Whole networks of Indigenous culture, of peasants, and direct producers develop an increasingly powerful counter-power at the grassroots level of society.

We do not expect – although it is not obviously not impossible – for counter-power to be destroyed in the short term. In any case, it would not be so easy to do so. Capitalist society has little or nothing to offer those who manage to constitute a sociability at the margins of its control and purely repressive solutions are costly from any point of view. However, the combination of co-optation and repression is always available.

It is possible to envision a coexistence, at the same time, of capitalist power (under whatever form it eventually acquires) and a counter-power that increasingly distances itself from open war and tends to affirm itself in its new productive and reproductive forms.

According to what we have developed so far, we can insist on two conclusions: 1) that capital must resolve (in Argentina) its dilemmas related to the forms of valorization and regulation of class struggle. The specific modalities of direct articulation between capital and the mafias is what is at stake at the moment. And this resolution is taking place in the context of the emergence of a counter-power of epic proportions. 2) Counter-power itself, in its development, must also resolve a number of fundamental questions in relation to the state, local governments, hunger, medicine, forms of self-management, connections between experiences, forms of self-defense, etc.

Thus, the fundamental axis of class struggle is configured by capital as control (and aspiration of control) of the productive *potencia* of the people and life and, on the other side, counter-power, as the tendency toward ever more autonomous reproduction of life. Their novel coexistence will not be without conflict.

9. **Capitalism produces men and women for death. The logic of confrontation, also maintained by sectors of the left, does so as well. The self-affirmation**

of *potencia* and multiplicity only exists as the will to persist and deploy life. Thus, we insist: to resist means to create (forms of life).

Class struggle is asymmetric. Capital plays the offensive. It conquers, colonizes. But it also, in a scandalous way, excludes and impoverishes. It is fundamental, in this respect, not to lose site of the fact that capital means control of *potencia* and of subjectivity, of nature and what is produced by science, and in general, the culture of the people.

Capital is nothing other than a social relation between humans and with nature. It is not possible to fight it as if it were external, as if it had its roots in government headquarters. The only way of combating capitalism, as the hegemony of sadness, exploitation, individualism, and the market, is through producing other forms of sociability, other images of happiness, another form of politics.

10. **In Argentina, and across Latin America, networks of production, anti-repression, counter-culture, alternative education and health care, and in general, for a radical politics that is no longer separated from life, are being developed. These networks, insofar as they tend to become autonomous from the command of capital and the state, offer new possibilities of developing the self-affirmation of the productive, cultural, and political *potencias* of autonomous experiences.**

The wager on making the reproduction of radical experiences increasingly autonomous requires practical hypotheses for its own project, as well as to be effectively implemented.

And from among what we have been saying, one thing stands out: in Argentina, there are a series of different – more or less diffuse, more or less organized – increasingly autonomous networks, related to barter, alternative economies, human rights, assemblies and public debates, others growing out of factory occupations (of which there are more than 200 now managed by their workers), others in health care, in education, and so on.

These experiences are very heterogeneous. Some are even, frankly, dark. But, at the same time, millions of people are *living* in them. In these experiences, political *punteros* and mafias connected to the state apparatus mix with the genuine expressions of vital reproduction for those who were considered dead, for years, by the capitalist market.

These networks tend toward autonomy with respect to capital's command to the same degree as they have lost any possibility of inclusion/integration in conditions that are minimally dignified. Or, in other words, to the extent to which desirable forms of inclusion are no longer available.

These networks have an enormous potential insofar as they put all of their resources into action: connecting producers to one another, producers with consumers, new forms of exchange without mafioso mediation, and especially, insofar as these circuits can sustain themselves by constructing mobile borders with the capitalist market.

11. **Power and counter-power can coexist for a long time without either one defeating the other. Power must solve its problems in order to persist, but counter-power must also develop its own solutions, which is no easy task. The central problem of this class struggle is, precisely, how to take on this conflictual coexistence.**

The coexistence of a capitalist power that is in a state of constant recomposition with a counter-power that is also constantly recomposing itself, creates anxiety for those who, on one side or the other, want to finish the game in a single move.

From the point of view of counter-power, it is vital to gain time, to strengthen these networks. There is an urgent need to develop a political theory that would allow for better understanding complex issues, such as relations between state institutions and grassroots politics, between struggles' effective presence and levels of representation, between situational leadership and *caudillismo*, between production and reproduction of life, between self-defense and exodus, between the necessary confrontations and protection of comrades and experiences, between local, national, and continental development, etc.

12. **The experiences of counter-power have consolidated greatly in the past few years. But they are being overwhelmed by an acceleration of time. No one is going to give them that time. Therefore, their virtue lies in the capacity to produce it. Militants in organizations of struggle could do so by also producing networks of autonomous material reproduction. And vice versa: the networks of autonomous reproduction, with all the ambiguities that envelop them, would undoubtedly benefit from a hybridization with the experience of the *piqueterx* struggle. The popular assemblies in various Argentinean cities could play a vitally important role of energizing these networks, as well as this encounter.**

The *piqueterxs* think of themselves as organizations of struggle. And they tend to seek alliances with other organizations of struggle. Nonetheless, from the point of view of a strategy of self-affirmation, this only covers one aspect of the experience: that of *confrontation*. If this line develops disproportionately in comparison to others, it will lead to a logic of confrontation. But if it is understood within the networks of counter-power as a whole, as a line that strengthens and protects, if it is developed as part of a work of composition with these economic, health, educational, and counter-cultural networks, it will encounter new perspectives, in the same way as it can open the doors to increasing the material foundations for building greater autonomy.

It is clear that this is not easy, because these networks are precarious. They still have not resolved all the basic issues and, in many cases, are infected with individualism and clientelism. Nonetheless, thinking about this dimension can create space for new alliances, experiences, and the production of new circuits. In this way, benefits can be obtained in the short term, such as affordable food (soy, rice, oil, etc.), generic medications (even creating their own laboratories), perhaps a school, a more effective coordinating body to counter repression, new spaces in which to discuss political theory, etc.

What is more, difficulty is probably related to the specific type of militancy that emerges as a model in these autonomous networks. It is no longer a specialist in ideologies or confrontations, but in situational operators of thought and skilled craftspeople of production and social reproduction. These are the categories of a new political theory of counter-power.

Of course, this is not easy. It is a hypothesis that must be taken to its final point. But there are good examples of experiences across the country, and across the continent, that support this path of development.

It is not a solution to all problems. Even repression itself will not disappear as a possibility. That is, that even working along this line, confrontation will be a harsh reality that must be addressed. But a new horizon can be glimpsed here: 1) the fusion of vital and political reproduction; 2) a better understanding of the possibilities for relations between representative institutions and grassroots experiences; and 3) avoiding the logic of confrontation to radically focus on self-affirmation.

C.S. July 2002

Conversation between Colectivo Situaciones and MTD Solano (Second round)[26]

1. Networks of counter-power

I think that the hypothesis about the *coexistence* – at least for a time, between a counter-power that grows from below and a power that tries to recuperate that space – is very risky. While it is true that we might think that neither of the two would be able to destroy the other, perhaps we need to define what those counter-powers are, how they are understood and how they exist, in order to analyze that coexistence, which would only be possible by distancing oneself from the war.

If we don't do that, it would be just as easy to think that the opposite would occur. Because while we want to distance ourselves from a direct and open confrontation, because we know that it would not be useful for us, the state thinks differently. The state will increasingly try to close the circle: the more we move away, the more it will harass us.

It is true that the forms of counter-power that are emerging tend to distance themselves from open war, because they are already aware of earlier experiences that demonstrate its inefficiency. But power has more than enough tools to drag us onto a battlefield, a place where they dominate, where they have all they need to win.

---

26 The conversations reproduced here are the product of five collective analysis workshops carried out in three different moments. The first eight points were recorded over three consecutive Fridays: July 19 and 26 and August 2. The ninth point was recorded on September 6 and the last three points emerged from a meeting that took place on October 11, as we were preparing for the publication of this book.

It is true that experiences of counter-power have the wisdom to try to avoid open war, because it is very easy to imagine who would win such a war. But what we wanted to talk to you all about is the place that piqueterxs occupy in that framework.

The hypothesis in question attempts to reflect on the existence of networks that work directly at the level of the reproduction of life and that at least tend to become independent from the power of the state and the demands of capital. These include all types of experiences and we don't necessarily have to like them all. Within this ocean of experiences, we can find the piqueterxs, who are those most linked to confrontation, not necessarily because of their vocation, but rather because of the role of benefits packages and the inevitable – contradictory and, to a certain extent, involuntary – relationship with the state. Other networks of counter-power do not necessarily have such an intense experience of struggle and, in that sense, it is interesting to think about the following point: that "organizations in struggle" – when they are understood as organizations that prioritize the element of physical confrontation (as often happens with the piqueterx movements) – do not encompass the multiplicity of aspects that are present in alternative networks, the many that you all experiment with...

But I also think that we can say that any experience that proposes working in the sense of counter-power is an experience of struggle because, regardless of the methodology and the different areas of construction, their work implies struggling against capitalism.

That is true, however there is a difference: some piquterx experiences tend toward direct confrontation while other alternative experiences express other variants (although it is clear that those also have to address, in their own way, problems related to confrontation). What we want to say is that the piqueterx struggle – up until now – seems to situate confrontation as a central element of the experience, while the issue does not come up in the same way in other experiences of counter-power.

It seems to me that we need to demystify our relation with the problem of violence, because it often appears grotesque. If we cover our faces, it is because the circumstances force us to do so, due to existing social and repressive violence. That is why they named us *piqueterxs*. The violence, then, is imposed by the system and we respond as we can, creatively. Because it is clear that creativity is the only thing that can save us from this war.

In any case, the problem appears in a particular way today, or at least that is how we perceive it. The major novelty seems to be that capitalism no longer has plans for a future integra-

tion of those who are currently "unemployed." If that integration were possible, repression would have a political significance that we are familiar with; that is, the repression would have a clear goal: making the rebellious workers go back to the factory, to production, to the working day, and making young people who don't work either go home or go to school. But we are left with the impression that it is difficult to understand this repression, because there are increasingly fewer factories to make the rebellious workers go back to... It seems that state violence, then, tries to stop the development of a counter-power that does not arise from the factory – except in the case of the employed – but from of experiences that attempt to produce and maintain alternative forms of life...

Yes, it is true that in the 1970s there was a type of militant that proposed something different to his or her comrades at work, another life: but workers earned 1200 pesos. They fought (in the factories) to defend their jobs.

2. Taking up the war in order to avoid it

Perhaps we have to return to the hypothesis that proposes a medium-term coexistence between a power that works by producing exclusion (or as we have been elaborating, "inclusion through exclusion") and a counter-power whose multiple forms of existence attempt to remove itself from this mechanism. Because it is not clear that counter-power will be able to eliminate the mechanisms of domination and solve everything – as the vanguardist left claims – if it gets into government tomorrow, nor can we expect (although it is not impossible) that capitalist power achieves all its goals, annihilating all the multiple experiences of resistance once and for all.

There are those who think that the social calamities that we are currently facing are caused by a passing crisis and that when everything returns to "normal" there will once again be employment, integration, without recognizing the extent to which current forms of capitalist accumulation are themselves mass producers of unemployment. If we add the experiences of the barter networks, community purchasing, alternative health care, it is difficult to see how they would be able to reproduce the same repressive mechanisms of the dictatorship.

But perhaps we have to recognize that these networks don't necessarily affect them. Because bartering, for example, is a network that operates according to market logics.

That is why we said initially that it is important to define what we mean by counter-power. It is obvious that the barter networks operate with capitalist elements, with value determined by supply and demand, with inflation, etc. I think that, in cultural terms, they reproduce the worst elements of capitalism and do not generate any type of counter-power, but rather reinforce the most perverse and miserable forms of this system in the most impoverished sectors. I would not consider them an experience of counter-power.

Here in Quilmes people buy sugar in peripheral nodes for three credits and they sell it in the Bernalesa[27] for three thousand: this is total speculation, and the Red Global cannot control it, because it is not a state or a force with the power to regulate. Then, it is even more liberal; the law of supply and demand is more savage. This is the total opposite of what I think of as counter-power.

I think that when you all speak of counter-power, you use the term too broadly. It seems as though everything that at some point emerged as distinct to power is necessarily in opposition to that power, and I don't think that it the case. Because often it is part of the same, because it does not always imply putting your body on the line to radically change society.

Confrontation can be understood in two different ways: as the conquest of power, as an offensive movement, or simply, as protection and self-defense of alternative forms of life. I think that the latter is what is interesting to us, because it corresponds to the practices of those of us who are involved in processes of the production of new values – not "moral values," but rather alternative practices. It is clear that there are many practices that have to defend what they think and produce, and perhaps we are not interested in all of them. But what is certain is that they have to face the same challenges of abandoning their previous certainties of what and how they do things to investigate what it is happening and how to resolve the problems that present themselves.

Regarding the barter networks, we do not know much about them, and undoubtedly, much of what you said is true, but we have been working for a while with some nodes that work fairly well – despite the fact that the current crisis has affected practically all the nodes in Buenos Aires – and we are seeing interesting things there. They are working a lot on using social bonds as an effective way of regulating exchange and production so as to avoid the things that you all were talking about. It is clear that all the nodes do not operate in the same way and, above all, that an experience that brings together three million people is not simple or pure, but a complex mixture of very diverse motives and dynamics.

In any case, it is not a matter of justifying the barter networks, but investigating which forms of alternative economies – from the many experiences that currently

---

27   The Bernalesa, the first barter club in Argentina, was founded on May 1, 1995. Located in Bernal, Quilmes, it is the biggest node in the country, and it functions as a central location and regulatory node of the Red Global del Trueque [Global Barter Network].

exist – are compatible with the material development of the experience of the MTDs, and with the economic activities that you all are carrying out. It would be absurd to say a priori that they are all compatible, but it would be even more absurd to say that none of them are, because that would stop us from searching.

This in no way is independent of the question we are discussing: the trap of confrontation. To the contrary, it has a lot to do with it. Because it is not the same to say that confrontation is a reality that we must engage with, considering it another element of the experience, one resource among others, as to place it at the center of our construction and believing that it will lead to all the solutions.

There are many options in this respect and perhaps we could present them in terms of three different modes of thinking. In the first, the solution lies in power. According to this perspective, everything that is being done now is more or less secondary to the extent that it does not lead, in a more or less direct way, to central power. Barter networks, for example, even in the case of nodes that manage to operate well, are nothing more that "the administration of misery," a factor that would even slow down "the real work."

Another mode of thinking believes that capitalism is going through a temporary crisis and will eventually integrate those who have momentarily been "excluded," based on the constitution of a more or less popular government.

And there is a third way of thinking, which is what we have been exploring. From this point of view, the question is about the possibilities of a counter-power that, in its concrete forms, can only expand by constantly asking itself about the problems that it is facing, the obstacles, the ways of resolving them, etc. From this perspective, it is clear that the solution cannot be focused on taking power, or exclusively on confrontation, but neither on the well-intentioned declaration that "everything will work out..."

But the fact is, precisely, that counter-power is nothing more than a series of very contemporary questions, practical questions that we have to be able to sustain, sort of like the Zapatistas do in very different circumstances. Among these questions, there is one that opens up the problem in a very material way, and this is the question related to the possibility of producing in an increasingly autonomous way, as a way to build independence – at least in relative terms – from the subsidies provided by the government.

One possibility would be to think that all of these experiences can do nothing other than reproduce capitalism from below, to the extent that they do not engage in a frontal and physical struggle with the government. However, even when it is true, this vision can end up closing paths that are worth exploring.

I was thinking that one of the most complicated problems we face in these places that have been most destroyed is that it is very difficult to avoid this direct friction with capitalism. Our situation is very complicated because there are no margins.

For example, we are thinking of occupying land, because, as you know, our sites are located in flood zones and we can't produce anything. Additionally, we are too crowded. The problem is that there is no land available, because the state sold all of it to make money: it is all private property. If you occupy land, they send in the army. As you don't have space, it is impossible not to clash with capitalism: that is why a degree of confrontation must necessarily exist. When you are wrapped up in this tension, sometimes you lose and sometimes you win, because it depends on the relations of force. There were twelve thousand people in the last land occupation here in Solano: there would have had to be a massacre to evict them. In those cases, the government is measured in its response, but in other cases they send in the bulldozers and that's that.

This is a problem for developing counter-power, for the possibilities of the autonomous reproduction of life: that the margins are increasingly narrow, and if we don't find a way to navigate them, it will be very difficult to advance. In Brazil, the Movimiento Sin Tierra (MST) found a way, but at a very high cost, because they were repressed at gunpoint, there were arrests and persecution, and there is still a lot of tension today. I don't know if we are going to be able to avoid that type of conflict with the state.

What can we do, for example, about the issue of land? Today we need land, not only to live on, but also in order to eat. It is obvious that the state will not give it to us. So, we are faced with a dilemma: how do we affirm ourselves, how do we develop a path that does not have to do with taking power, but with the creation of new values, that also requires affirming the defense of life? I sincerely don't know how we can do it.

It is true that one runs up against power even if one is not seeking it out. And we don't make confrontation with the state a central element of what we do. But if you touch private property, they will send the army, the judges... In other words, while capitalism exists, we are going to clash with one of its forms. Now, well, the issue is that for us, the economic element is not the central focus: our struggle is for a different life in which the economic aspect is only one part. The struggle for social change must be comprehensive.

We don't imagine that the dilemma is about building hippie communities, nor that piqueterxs will solve their problems by isolating themselves with the hopes of finally living in peace – which is, on the other hand, an illusion that we might all have. If one thing is clear, it is that it is not easy. Furthermore, the problem of violence should not be posited in a moral or abstract way. To the contrary, if posed concretely, in most cases, it is a necessity of the struggles. Therefore, it is not about judging, but of asking if the path of struggle – that, we insist, always implies a degree of violence – does not unfold better when it does not fall into the game of war. If, as we think, developing a war against capital in the current circumstances would lead to losing it, perhaps we could say that taking on the war means, in turn, avoiding the prioritization of the moment of open confrontation.

Without escalating the war, we have to think about and build self-defense. In the Aníbal Verón Coordinator, we have talked a lot about the fact that we are in a stage of resistance, of resistance to a single way of thinking and resistance to a tremendous degradation in values. This part is the most messed up, because it is not only a matter of hunger, but also, and especially, the degradation of the human being as a whole. We are worried because many people are thinking in terms of a pre-revolutionary situation. There are people who are living in the past and think that the situation is mature and the only thing missing is the vanguard that will take power and produce the revolution from above.

3. Power of the ideal or a real movement

Another problem that I see with what was posited in terms of the possibilities of coexistence between counter-power and power is that as long as that counter-power does not nourish and produce other subjectivities and values, they could destroy us by taking out a group of militants. Then it would be followed by forms of struggle for subsistence itself, people will raid supermarkets, will go out to steal, etc. In other words, does this not lead us to the traditional question: the worse, the better?

Let's think about it another way. If we identify counter-power only with people who are thinking about an ideal of another society, we are stuck in a very weak, very ideological, situation. Perhaps the question could be formulated differently: Are there not already experiences that no longer exclusively feed off of the identifying images and requirements supplied by capitalism? And, if these experiences that are producing in another register – even if they have no idea of what socialism would be, as in our case – exist in different spheres of society, it is very possible that, building off of all those phenomena, "something else" is already emerging. The value of that something else is not given, in effect, by its capacity to produce representative, symbolic, theoretical forms, but rather by its ability to keep the experiment open: the expansiveness of counter-power as such. Perhaps then, instead of "uniting the socialists," it would be more interesting to create connections with the experiences that make up "points of potencia," of experimentation, to see how we can connect and expand together.

We are convinced, in this respect, that an "idea," as an ideal, is always going to be weaker than everyday lived experience. Therefore, it is difficult to fight capitalism only with ideas, because capitalism is not an idea, but a reality, and an extremely resistant one at that. That is why having "pure ideas" is never enough, but rather we have to constitute experiences, values, ways of thinking, and practical images of happiness that are able to compete with and even surpass capitalism's enormous capacities. Of course, these experiences do not have the purity of the idea. But they surpass it in their desirability, their potencia, in reality. Then, it is not so much a case of "the worse the better" – as certain elements of Marxism thought insist – but rather that as Marx and his friend Engels warned, the "real movement" does not need to "adjust" to any "ideal." When one becomes very insistent on the ideal, they can start insisting on molds, which only function to format and constrain the real movement.

Yes, I remember when a comrade from the MST in Brazil came here and we carried out a popular education workshop, in which some comrades said that a big part of our crisis as an organization was that we did not have a clear, articulated political project, that would define a program. And the comrades from the MST told us that they have been around for 25 years as an organization and that if you were to ask many of the founding members what socialism is, they would have no idea. In fact, if that were the motive for their project, surely not very many people would mobilize for it. But if you tell people in a settlement that there is a land occupation, that the comrades need help so that they can start to work, a huge number of people would mobilize. Why? Because they experience it in their daily lives, and that is socialism, that exists in practice and not as a system of defined, programmed, dogmatic ideas.

Of course, the big problem with working subjected to an ideal is that it ends up obstructing the possibility of encountering possible alternatives in one's own experience. As we know, both in regards to what one proposes, and when one has clear goals, the only thing that needs to be done is to accommodate real experience – lived experiences – to those knowledges that would bring us closer to the ideal. There is no creativity or real experience there. But the critique of that mode of thought involves putting into practice another mode of subjectivity that has more to do with the capacity for investigation based on existing practices and the possibilities that they provide, about the forms of sociability that emerge in those practices, which we do not know too much about beforehand.

What seems extremely important to us in this sense is that it is only these real practices that can be resources for our own projects. Because they can respond to question:

How is it possible to produce the resources that we need to develop this counter-power in the current circumstances? In other words, in order to think new things, it is necessary to think differently. That "other way of thinking," we believe goes beyond what we usually think of as "politics." For example, if confrontation is understood based on traditional modes of politics, it necessarily implies the question of power, relations of force, ultimately, the subordination and reorganization of life under the requirements of that confrontation. But, would it be possible to think about it in another way?

When we talk about these networks that are emerging, we realize that they do not think in the ways we are used to, they do not think "politically." Nonetheless, it is obvious that they think, because they find solutions, even if only partial solutions, for a wide variety of problems. It seems as though there is a great affinity between the experiences of a new protagonism, at least from a certain perspective: they do not separate politics *from* life.

That is why for us it is surprising when you say that the barter networks reproduce capitalism: does that not also happen in the piqueterx movement in some way?

We have often said here that capitalism is not external to the MTD. Furthermore, for someone who knows other piqueterx organizations (like D'Elia's): would you say that they don't reproduce capitalism there?

Thus, it is important to also think differently about the assembly movement. Because the most interesting things tend to be those that are least visible, what is not easily seen: incipient experiences, that start to reorganize certain circuits in the neighborhood. However, there is often an attempt to see them as authentic soviets, or they are elevated when they demonstrate a certain capacity to mobilize, to organize marches to Plaza de Mayo every Friday, but people are generally not capable of seeing beyond these elements.

Undoubtedly, these forms of sociability that are appearing and expressing another becoming are not easy to see or to accompany. Now, if counter-power does not attempt to take a sharper look, with more humility, more connected to the real possibilities offered by the real movement, that is, if it does not modify its perception and way of thinking, it is clear that it will do nothing other than repeat the same paths as always.

4. Beyond politics

It is true that five years ago, we all still thought that solution would have some sort of institutional form. Now many opportunities have opened up, which does not mean that the crisis will come to an end. But what matters is that we are searching and that is a welcome change. Before, these conversations only took place in parliament buildings, city councils, or municipal governments. In that since, the barter networks are a search, an attempt to resolve problems differently from the way that capitalism does not solve them. Despite all their problems, we must think about it as a process, that perhaps will evolve into something good. For example, if they manage to directly connect the nodes with the producers of flour, rice, etc., perhaps they could put a stop to the speculation practiced by those who go to make deals, because those harm the producers as well. In other words, they are engaging in a search, and it is only to be expected that it would be traversed by human misery, because that is what we are enmeshed in, and from which we are seeking to escape in any way possible. But it is a possibility that, if it is developed, could be very interesting.

It also has to do with a more general process that has been going on in the neighborhoods for a few years. In fact, I started doing things in my fourth year of high school, when I got together with a group of kids and it was an apolitical group. It was a very valid experience; we went through a number of things and we learned from them. But I think that while there was a need to form an apolitical group, unconsciously we were on a path toward the political. Because ultimately being apolitical is a good way of doing politics.

This can also be seen in other experiences such as that of the Movimiento Campesino de Santiago del Estero (MOCASE, Peasant Movement of Santiago del Estero). They started the movement ten years ago without a specific political ideology. It is an experience that could be called "apolitical," but that a very radical nature, perhaps not because it is "apolitical," but due to developing "beyond politics."

Clearly, a naive demand toward authority is not the same type of anti-politics as an experience of self-construction based on the resources and values that exist in the compañeros in a place. The latter means working on a deep level that politics does not reach, because it implies trusting in our own resources, our own thinking, in the capacities of our compañeros. It is on this level that a social fabric is being generated that is precisely the relationship that capitalism constantly destroys, turning us into individual subject to power. The difference between these two forms of critiquing politics lies in self-organization. In this sense, it is a matter of a "beyond" what is usually understood as politics and integrates other dimensions of existence.

It is not a matter of relative, temporary autonomy, something that is done "in the meantime," as we wait for something else. Rather, this is the only real moment, and the only space for thinking: in the last instance, socialism is nothing other than a moment of comprehensive self-organization, is it not?

So, a group that does not participate in this dynamic of self-production of the social is a group that can have pure "ideas" about how the world "should be" and once again the issue of the mold, or model, appears.

This has nothing to do with what is happening today, with the unfolding of experiences that are able to organize themselves outside the requirements of capital valorization. These are symptoms of the reorganization of society, even if there is still no coherent discourse that accounts for this and if these phenomena are also mixed with the worst elements of capitalism.

Ultimately, we can find more potencia and multiplicity in these experiences – even in the most problematic ones – than in all the "good ideas," which are often nothing more than pure ideals. It seems to us that it is an especially interesting moment to develop searches in that field of experience.

Most intellectuals and politicians think that this is provisional, corresponding to a more or less temporary crisis, but we need to examine it closely to see if that is the case. Thinking differently, however, could also mean, no longer talking about ourselves based on lack: the piqueterx nuclei that started organizing themselves, the first barter nodes, and a school such as Creciendo Juntos produce a new subjectivity that operates and generates effects in their surroundings. Rather than lack, then, we could think about the desire for social bonds. The crisis is no longer a simple temporary moment, but rather, it implies a contradictory becoming in which, on the one hand, the weakness of capitalist hegemony is perceived, but, at the same time, the effects of the crisis also tend to attack those experiences that are being consolidated. But we could also hypothesize that the project is based on the desire for another life supported by autonomous forms of social bonds, as much as on the crisis.

One of the big problems that society has had is thinking that we are building all of this in order to arrive at something else. That vision was always part of a human fallacy, that of having to put labels on everything. For us, counter-power, at least as we understand it and have talked about it, does not have a defined goal to which to arrive, it is not programmed, we make it by traveling together. We cannot assume that we have to mechanistically transfer what the MST does in Brazil or the EZLN in Chiapas to Buenos Aires. We are in very different contexts. Perhaps they are further from the center of power, but the system attempts to annihilate them just the same, whether they construct counter-power or propose taking power.

I think that it would be a mistake to posit that we deploy counter-power in order to build "socialism." We build counter-power to change this shitty reality. It is something for today, and tomorrow we will continue building to change tomorrow's shitty reality. And we don't know where we will end up.

5. Alternative economics and the crisis

I think what you all were saying before – that the crisis is not what is driving these experiences – is debatable. I think it is a little different here, because many people are interested in the movement because they can't find solutions anywhere else. The crisis is what made some people participate in the roadblocks. The other day I was talking to a comrade who said: "Look, I was someone who lived for my job, I woke up at three or four in the morning, I went to the Capital, I returned at night. My idea was to get ahead, build a house, give the best to my children, and all those things within the idea of progress, of getting ahead. But I was a terrible slave. That was my life. Now I might not be doing well in economic terms, but I discovered my family, the neighborhood, what it means to be together, sharing things, now I feel a little bit freer." In that way, the crisis was a slap in the face for many people.

Of course, because is often depicted as a purely economic crisis, when, in reality, it is a crisis of meaning. In the Creciendo Juntos School,[28] for example, they clearly perceive how the – deep – crisis of public school made them think about certain precautions, certain forms of work, but the driving force behind their project is not found in the lack brought about by the crisis, but in the intense desire linked to the production of social bonds, in this case, connected with education.

But, at the same time, the effects of this crisis of meaning are paralyzing more than anything else. You go from having to wake up every day at six in the morning to go to work, to the idea that "now there is no one to tell me what to do, so now I will do what I want." This is a problem, and it kills me, because when I get to the neighborhood, everyone is sitting around drinking mate and if there is nobody to tell them how to do things, they don't do anything. This worries me a lot.

There is also the issue of being flexible with the comrades, not using punishments, and instead resolving everything in assemblies, talking together. The truth is that it's fine, but there are people who are used to having someone tell them what to do, and suddenly here, when they are in a group, they have a certain level of responsibility and they want things run with an iron fist. Or the feeling that being in the movement, being a delegate, means gaining prestige: "I do politics, I don't work." The other day, chatting with the leader of an important Latin American social movement and I asked him if he was based in any particular place, and he answered: "no, we are militants."

---

28   Creciendo Juntos is an educational community located in the municipality of Moreno in the urban periphery of Buenos Aires. See *Borradores de investigación 2: Sobre el conocimiento inútiil,* Colectivo Situaciones 2001.

Nonetheless, our biggest problem is how to get through this moment, how to solve problems and grow, while also avoiding the state; how to go about achieving greater degrees of real autonomy. Because the problem is that we have a relative, restricted autonomy, and this leaves us with a very high degree of exposure. The state still has us on a leash: the benefit packages and subsidies. However, within the movement, we can think about and construct autonomy. Autonomy does not only mean gaining independence from the state or from superstructures, autonomy is also achieved on the personal, group, political, and social levels.

It is the complex situation of precarity that stops us from taking the next step. We really are exposed, and we are not just anywhere, but in the heart of power: an urban area strongly marked by all the dynamics of power. It is different in the countryside, where comrades have land, and where instituting collective work should not be as difficult; although we know about the bulldozers, the judges, and all that.

This is, without a doubt, one of the more interesting problems that has emerged in recent months, and it is a field of work that has opened up a lot after the 19th and 20th. But we are missing practical hypotheses to deal with these problems: How can we generate effective networks between experiences that are producing their own resources as a way of starting to project an autonomous future in the economic, material realm, in terms of subsistence as well? This is not to say that there is an immediate solution that will save us from the state's leash, but to make it possible for initiatives that are able to further diversify projects to emerge, so that at least the leash will not be the only source of resources.

Yes, that is the path of the possible development of a project of autonomy.

Then we can return to the question of how we perceive counter-power and, therefore, with which experiences it would be worth initiating a process of encounter, exchange, and collective work. In this sense, thinking about counter-power based on a set of ideological definitions is not the same as understanding it as the development of experiences that are practically working on projects that have a logic that differs from that of capital, even if we do not have a good understanding of what that logic is, nor can we see its future.

For example, we were talking to a friend who is a pharmacist and a group of his friends who just opened a pharmacy providing generic medications, and they have the technical conditions to build – at any moment – a laboratory to produce the medication themselves. That is one example of what can be done: autonomously produce good quality and affordable medication, with legal recognition.

There are many others like them – and some of the barter nodes are an incredible laboratory in this sense – that are inventing ways of re-appropriating and initiating processes built on existing productive capacities. These are capacities that capital has not taken advantage of and that can be re-articulated, by a dynamic that is neither that of a state bureaucracy or the market. It is, if you will, what happens in some of the worker-recuperated factories. They are militants, but they don't think like traditional militants that are only concerned with the problem of taking power. They try to forge a new type of protagonism and, to do so, it is essential to intervene in the affinities and possibilities of effective composition.

Because when you all develop a project like that of the alternative school: What does it mean that it not just you all organizing, but also, some teachers, a group of architects, and some neighborhood residents? One way of thinking about it, that is perhaps the most obvious, is that "people are in solidarity with us because we struggle, because we are a new reference point or political hope…" But we could also think that what is happening is that we are seeing an enormous available potential, a new protagonism that unfolds transversally throughout the social body and is seen in a ton of places, and that can be interlinked in multiple ways. It is obvious that these are two different ways of thinking.

We see very clearly this difference between conceptions. Fighting for benefits from the government with strict guidelines on what is considered important, the political struggle, is not the same as fighting to recover the capacity to do things, to organize ourselves. The first is more abstract: we accumulate a thousand benefit packages because, with those, we will support the two hundred militants that will be needed to carry out the revolution tomorrow. That is not what happens here: what we want is, precisely, to build this network of alternative production. Because that is the way to escape the government's grip, there is no other way. Even if we were to have Marx and Engel among us, the only way to continue the project is to loosen the state's leash.

We insist again: what matters is what happens in the MTD and not its relation with the state. Because ultimately, we don't have to depend on the state but we might still depend on the market logic. The fight with the state and a certain dependence for demands is not the essential element for the MTD. What matters is what we do, how we organize these demands, what use we put them toward, what values we work with, and what type of sociability will come from our practices. Because what matters is that each comrade chooses to be in the MTD and it is not that they feel obligated due to economic necessity.

I think that this is what is important and this is how we want to build the movement. What happens is that we are not used to thinking of ourselves as an experience, as an organization. To be honest, we often don't think that way. That is where our work lies: thinking about how we can get away from the state. The day that we have the capacity to build a network and deploy autonomous production, we will say: "take this and stick it up your ass, now we will do things differently."

I don't know if it's like that, because we will not be able to develop something of that magnitude by ourselves: it is more a matter of searching and being open to others. What we have is something to give, and therefore we can come together with other people and share things. Maybe it will take years to be able to do many of the things we want to do; maybe others have interesting experiences that we can learn from. If we sustain our work, surely, we will build relationships that will strengthen our movement.

One thing that someone sees immediately when they go to a school like Creciendo Juntos is that the children and their families do not come together with the same beliefs of a traditional school. They participate because they like to do so and not because they have no choice. The question then, continuing with the example, is knowing what would happen if these networks of alternative production and distribution were developed: is it possible that at some point a person who is working twelve hours a day for three hundred or four hundred pesos will be able to perceive that they can live in a way that is much more interesting in these networks?

6. The offensive, the vanguard, the desire for stardom...

We wanted to talk with you all about how you feel and think about the fact that people are increasingly identifying and taking into account the MTDs and the Aníbal Verón Unemployed Workers' Coordinator. In other words, how you feel about suddenly becoming "famous." We see it as a contradiction, because the MTDs (and the Aníbal Verón) never deploy a vanguardist discourse, they don't look for people to follow them; it does not seem like this is just another chapter in the history of the emergence of political vanguards, but rather a more "communicative" phenomenon, tied to the media, images... It is further complicated by the fact that the Verón appears as a new source of hope for the left. For many on the non-partisan left – because parties are in competition with you all – the MTDs appeared as a solid organization, with a more creative line of thought and that fights hard; but many of the most interesting and deepest things about the MTDs do not appear, they remain hidden in that powerful image. That is, a capacity of struggle appears, but taken up in a somewhat artificial way. There is a risk that that level of expectations and identification turns into pressure on the MTDs, is there not?

That's exactly how it is. In fact, within the Verón there are groups that completely assume that role, and say: "now is the moment," "we are playing in division one," "we have to be more careful." That is not how we see it. At the moment, our first obligation, our priority, is to work within the organization to elaborate everything that has happened to us, to be able to understand and evaluate it. Obviously, we devoted some time to the media's demands, because they had thrown so much shit at us and we had to take advantage of this tool to share our own words. But that does not mean ignoring what is fundamental: elaboration with our comrades, the work that has to be taken up. We are very clear about this to the comrades who are in a hurry: there is no use in being left with thirty very brave people and a much larger number of people asking "what happened?" We are not a vanguard organization; we are a popular organization that has its own temporality and rhythm and we struggle together with all of our comrades. Unfortunately, there have been moments when we have had to make immediate decisions without carrying out the discussion process that we are used to, because, especially after June 26, we were operating in a very complex context, full of urgent situations. That is what just what happened to us. But that does not mean that we are going to leave behind all our comrades, the elaborations, the debates.

It is no coincidence that groups in the Verón are proposing that it is time to create a group of comrades that would be able to make decisions in certain situations. "Hierarchalize the environment" is the term that is used, and it means that the best players should go on the field for the coordinator. It is what provokes acceleration. But we are all very round, it will be difficult to fit us in a square hole, it will be difficult to make a cadre organization out of us.

Precisely, you hear them saying, "we have to go on the offensive," as if we were still on the "defensive," that is, doing nothing more than surviving the punches and the whole discussion should be posited in terms of how to now go on the "attack." The "offensive," however, is an ambiguous expression because while, on the one hand, it points to the – desirable – abandonment of pure withdrawal; on the other hand, at the same time, it is a military metaphor that ends up identifying more with the doctrine of invading, imperialist armies, with the objective of conquering distant lands, than with the popular resources that effectively count. We can see that in some of the organizations from the 1970s, can we not? The strategic offensive can become an illusion that stops, in concrete terms, having the people's will and resources: it would give the impression that those resources are available, instead, on the defensive. In the theory of war, the weak possess resources for defense (multitude, knowledge and management of the territory, etc.) and the strong are those who go on the offensive: those who manage to select a group of specialized people, arm them, to take control of others' resources. That was a big debate in the 1970s.

The problem is that those groups end up being the hook that makes the state come for us. They go out and say idiotic things on television and they leave us with the mess. One question we ask them: do you have what you need to do that? Furthermore: Where were you on December 20, those of you who talk about the great uprising of the people? But they are the ones who think, not those who do, that is why they have to protect themselves. That is why they say: "You have to go out to fight, but some of us have to organize."

It is true that the offensive is the logic posited by the enemy and this what led to the comrades' defeat in the 1970s: the conception that a confrontation pitting apparatus against apparatus is necessary. It is difficult to avoid because many people often have the desire to do so. When they killed Darío and Maxi, some people asked: "How long are they going to continue killing our people?" That "how long" is really asking: "when are we going to start doing it?" On the other hand, physical disappearance is not the only thing that destroys projects; capitalism establishes itself on many planes.

They don't only kill us during the roadblocks; they kill us in the neighborhoods with unemployment, misery, and left-wing parties also kill us: with defamation, by placing inappropriate demands on us.

This especially has to do with the ambiguity in the discussion about self-defense. Defending different existing modes of life, protecting experiences that are being constructed with another logic (that is not the logic of war), is not the same as thinking about self-defense as a superior form of struggle, as a step toward the offensive. The problem is that this tension exists on the material plane, not only as distinct ideas, but as real dynamics that organize the forces of counter-power. When confrontation is made central – as an exclusionary logic – that experience starts to displace other efforts, directing them toward things that do not provide an autonomous, self-affirmative becoming. Problems are always presented to us as "decisive" but, in reality, they are only one more element of the multiplicity of existing resources and problems.

Therefore, the struggle can also be taken up in another way, avoiding the reproduction of a logic purely organized by confrontation, displacing other elements that are equally fundamental.

That is why it is impressive what Zapatismo has done: after that huge march to Mexico City, in which the entire society mobilized and the whole country began to discuss the Indigenous issue, they returned to their communities and called for silence.

After that, they did not address anyone. Of course, there are those who say that by doing so they leave the terrain open for president Fox and the right.

This complaint is always made by those who cannot sustain what they want for themselves, and they complain or blame others.

We are going through something similar to what happened to the comrades from Mosconi, who were on the news when there were deaths [*piqueterxs* killed by police forces] and one month later nobody cared about them. The same thing is going to happen here. Our plan is to continue doing what we have been doing, but also to address the people who want to get to know us and learn about what we do. If they invite you to an assembly, you have to go and create a relationship. But you have to be careful to never lose sight of your main idea, because if we start spending more time visiting assemblies than on our own work, then we are screwed. In fact, we don't choose specific comrades for those things. We do what we can with what is available. Our main work is here and we cannot lose sight of that because it would be very hypocritical and deceitful. I think the problem is when you believe what the media or those others say, or when they make you believe it.

When you believe it, you move onto another plane of existence, you start frequenting other circuits, having other needs and other problems.

You go from being the Verón to being the "representative" of a broad sector of society, and therefore, they expect you to do something in the name of society. When they ask us "and what is the Verón going to do?" they are trying to put us in the position of representation. The problem of accepting this "representation" is what would be lost. If we get angry and decide that this is the moment to go on the offensive, we will destroy everything we have.

But it is hard to make us buy into the discourse of the vanguard, because we know very well that there are fifty million problems in the neighborhood and we don't even have four solutions for them. It is one thing that the media inflates what you do, and something very different in the everyday life of the neighborhood. That is why we invite everyone who wants to learn about the movement to look at it from the inside.

7. The experience of pain

But there are not only demands coming from the left, but also from the right.

What are the demands by the right?

When they say "you have to seriously rethink the roadblocks, the masks, the methods that you use." And they also say that we lead people to death. But what happened did not fit into any analysis: the repression that we suffered on June 26 surpassed any capacity of analysis.

Yes, there is the issue of recognition, no one wants to appear stupid. But there is also the possibility of going deeper and moving beyond the terms imposed by the media. What are the real perspectives and how can we work so that we are not drawn into that game? One of the topics that came up several times in the workshop, which you all clearly articulated, was: How to resolve the issue of dependency on the state?

It is a very complicated issue. Today, the type of autonomy we want, in the context of the life that we have, is impossible. It is not even possible for the people in the movement. The situation we are in, of a lot of misery and lack of resources, leads you to say: "either we die of hunger in the neighborhood or we die in a march or in a roadblock." Death is already established here, in many senses. For example, if you go to the hospital, they give you an appointment for three months from now, or a kid is burned and there is nothing to treat him with. In this context, it is very difficult to think about alternatives that do not include making demands on the state.

This cannot be denied. Effectively, the issue is twofold: on one side, demanding state funding for the services that are delegated to it, and, on the other, developing a line of construction in the medium and long term based on counter-power's own resources. If this second struggle is not possible, the first – calling for the state to fulfill the functions that it used to carry out, including the most basic ones – will also be frustrated. First, because it tends to be the second of those struggles that allows for better results in the first. And, second, because all of our efforts would go to that first struggle, which would not leave us with capacities to take up the tasks required by the experience of autonomy and, finally, because in those conditions, it is easy for subordination to the mechanisms of power to be exacerbated.

If we are going based on what we have managed to do up to now, it must be said that this problem has consumed us in many moments, it tied us up and left us without the capacity for other types of responses. But we continue our work: productive projects, political education, etc. The central axes defining our practice from the beginning – "struggle, political education, and work" – have not been lost. Today we are working with a lot of people, attempting to build our own school, planning a new land occupation, exploring possibilities of connecting with comrades from other countries; we have the bakery and we are starting our own gardens.

We have thought a lot about the possibility of making a call to turn inward – in the Zapatista style – and consolidate this type of peace, which I don't know how long will last. We do not have to be oriented by the rhythm of the conjuncture. We need our own times, because struggling based on the temporalities proposed by the enemy is to struggle on the enemy's' field and with their weapons. We have to have our own weapons, our own terrain, and our own time. Ceding any of these would mean getting trapped in a form of struggle imposed by the enemy, responding to the steps that they identify. Breaking with this requires turning inward and managing our own times. We will go more slowly, we will arrive later, we will miss the train, but we will all be together.

This also means escaping from that choice that, as you were saying before, is imposed on you: the choice between dying of hunger in the neighborhood and dying heroically in a march.

Yes, because if those are the choices, then we don't have a logic of life. Instead, the choice has to be thought of in terms of choosing how to live.

Nonetheless, the death of Darío hit us all very hard: because of our relationship with him. And the everyday experience of pain also hits us hard: women here are giving birth to malnourished babies, because they were malnourished in the womb. That weighs hard on us, that coexistence with death.

What we are experiencing will also require a very profound reflection so that we are not taken advantage of. There is real need: we are not going to be able to stop struggling, and we are going to keep struggling in a setting in which many different interests intersect. Thus, there is a risk of instrumentalization. We will need intelligence, reflection, wisdom to not be pulled in by those interests. Today repression comes from different groups that are operating at full force to make certain things happen. In that sense, everything is much more complex. Because you cannot simply say, "the government is the enemy." No, there are gangs that no longer respond to an institutional line, but rather operate based on their own interests in a completely inorganic way. There we find a very dangerous issue. Because while we see that, to a certain extent, society supports us, that some media outlets behave well, we have the sensation that that is not enough. We have to be very careful to not end up getting trapped. It is very difficult to think of effective forms of protection today.

8 An investigation without a model

It would be good to deepen our perception of other experiences that are emerging in the search for alternative forms of resolving problems of existence. Obviously, it would be stupid to believe that all these experiences immediately have a common goal. However, it would also be absurd to refuse to connect with the flow of social doing due to excessive caution, would it not? We already talked about the risks of a type of purity politics, that does not take into account what is happening within those experiences of counter-power, which are always very contradictory...

Yes, I think there is a little pessimism that often creates obstacles to establishing connections. The other day, we were debating over the Coordinadora de Organizaciones Populares Autónomas [Coordinator of Autonomous Popular Organizations, COPA], and we could see that many militants would go there looking for a name, a flag. But we could also see that if we look for a space that meets all of the conditions that we want, then, undoubtedly, we will find ourselves very alone in Argentina. This requires work, because the contradictions are not only found in certain sectors of society, but they are also present in our neighborhoods. In the most impressive struggles that we have at the grassroots level, you can also find capitalist categories.

It would be a big mistake to abandon the search and the free nature that sharing these spaces should have. We have to look for encounters in all spheres, there is no privileged sphere in that sense. Still, we would never go out to recruit people, but we are interested in sharing spaces. Of course, there are times that you go and come back thinking that you did not get anything out of it. Sometimes you are left with a sensation that it was a waste of time, because it was not productive. But resolving this by simply giving up would be the easier thing to do, because you fall into prioritizing principles that lead you to think that you should only connect with those who are most advanced, those who think like we do.

The same thing happens during assemblies. There are some people who have changed and overcome their conditions, but others who are still thinking in terms of money, of their bank accounts. But, if we were to reject them a priori, because they are the "limits of the petty bourgeoisie," we would be doing nothing other than putting a label on them and closing the blinds on a space that could potentially generate something new. I think that generally expresses the prevailing pessimism.

But I think that it is more than pessimism and it has to to do with a conception that implies that we already know where we are going and what we want. Then, all that we have to do is build it, in other words, just going up. But it is a very different perspective when one looks to the sides, because it involves considerable work of investigation that starts from the acknowledgment that we don't know where we are going and that demands sustained experimentation...

Sometimes what is missing there is that fresh air of searching, of creating, of existing. Sometimes there is something like exhaustion, lack of belief, a rationalism that brings us to abandon spaces because you start elaborating something and it doesn't work out. The issue is that it has to do with a way of thinking that doesn't take into account the newness that can arise from an encounter in which something different might emerge, but rather judges based on fairly dogmatic criteria.

This is important, because it requires you to constantly re-elaborate things and not reject anything a priori, because the new can also arise from the old. Nothing is born pure. As long as there is capitalism, we will always be co-existing, and no experience will be one hundred percent in agreement with what we wish or desire. This goes for everyone: the unemployed, the assemblies, the barter clubs. In all of them there will be people who are making an effort to do something different and not only speculate with merchandise to get one more credit. That is what is difficult: not placing labels on things. This also happens frequently with the university sector, but there are also people in it who are searching. Some comrades think that you can't do anything with those university students and that they should be left to the system, to the businesses. However, we have had very enriching experiences working with students.

Basically, we are talking about the question of how to autonomously produce the material foundations for counter-power. This also has a lot to do with the question of how to avoid confrontation, because you can decide that confrontation is not the central element, and even be very conscious about that, but if it is not possible to stop depending on state benefits – which, in turn, depend on the ability to carry out roadblocks – it will not be easy to escape the logic of confrontation.

That is why we think it is so important to work on the issue of the networks of material reproduction that are emerging in our country: with food, medicine, culture, communication, alternative politics, education, economies. Perhaps these experiments cannot completely replace the benefit packages – which might seem like a fantasy today – but they could be useful for strengthening the movement's productive enterprises and workshops, so that the benefits and confrontation with the state are no longer the only resource available, are no longer exclusively in the center of the project.

If it is possible to recognize that there are more possibilities to fall back on, more potential resources, than what we are used to perceiving, then confrontation can become something that we start to choose tactically, rather than something that is imposed on us.

From there we also saw a problem: a militant whose only job is consciousness and confrontation are not the same as the militant who is a producer of a networks. This distinction has important implications in the wake of June 26, especially if you believe that we are not in a revolutionary situation in which taking power would be an option. That is why we postulated the hypothesis we discussed, that of a (at least in the short and medium term) coexistence between power and counter-power, with aggressive, repressive forms of power. Undoubtedly, power has hypotheses of reproduction, and our problem seems to be: what is counter-power's hypothesis of material reproduction?

This has to do with how the issue of autonomy is understood: if autonomy is defined only by the capacity to fight and be able to self-manage certain projects, establishing an independence from the state that allows us to carry out certain tasks, or if autonomy has to do with a project that goes much further. That is where it would be interesting to delve deeper: What does it means to be an autonomous popular movement and what horizon does that lay out for us? In that sense, this relation, that coexistence with the state, with the enemy, is simply circumstantial and not primordial, and what is ultimately fundamental is that we have the capacity to build.

I think this is a very important point. Because for many groups, their horizon is very clear: a model of socialism in which they know what it is and how they will build it when they get there, a plan that extends from the present into a determined number of years in the future. There are other groups that have a model of integration: for them, the horizon is to return to a Peronist state in which there would be redistribution, labor with dignity, social services, etc. But it is more difficult for counter-power experiments because they have to invent, create something that is never fully and clearly defined, because it is a road that has to be traveled on, with a certain degree of uncertainty.

However, to me, it is very important that in that question about the horizon that we don't turn to imaginary inventions, but that we examine experiences that already have a material existence, that we develop what exists today as seeds (which of course are ambivalent) of new modes of life.

The dilemma lies in what to do to be able to produce our own time that would allow us to carry out this practical investigation about the alternative networks taking shape, how they are being produced and producing, with whom we can carry out that investigation. It must be difficult for the MTD to be able to take distance from the thousands of everyday problems: the benefit packages, the bureaucratic paperwork, coordinating the action plans, all types of meetings, constantly receiving visitors, right?

Yes. As a project, we can't say that we have a large degree of freedom. Often, we can't find spaces for reflection. Most of the emergencies happen in our action plans, dealing with this or that mess, submerged in a flood.

Nonetheless, I think that the comrades have made considerable advances, especially when I see that they join a project for reasons besides just receiving benefits. That is where we can see that there is effectively a purging of much of the capitalist shit that we carry with us. But there is no doubt that this new way of living, and of understanding what we want, takes place in a setting of a lot of tension, in which things are mixed together.

Sometimes we even start having illusions and think that we are experiencing something that we are not, especially in comrades who have been working for a long time. There are times when you have to burst the bubble, and to do so, you have to stop, catch your breath, and think, because if not, you get wrapped up in everything going on. It's horrible.

I agree with what you are saying. As long as we can't manage to shake off this collar of the state, it is going to be difficult to increase the spaces of freedom. Because that is what the state does to us, it throws us here, it spins us around there: one day it closes doors for you, the next day it opens them, one day it gives you something, the next day it takes it away. We know that we are wearing this collar and that one day we are going to have to break it. That does not mean quitting the struggle or giving up, but rather recognizing that, as organizations, we are very exposed, very fragile, and that we have to take precautions if really want to fully escape this.

Furthermore, this has to arise from a collective reflection and the agreement of the entire movement. It can't be the decision of a small group of comrades who are aware of certain things and sit down to deepen their understanding. We have to find a way for the whole movement to take part in this process. The other day we were talking with a group of comrades and it was very clear that December marked a turning point, and that, at least for us, June was also a turning point. In that sense, we are left with a lot of work to figure out how to reorganize ourselves in this new situation, to maintain this horizon that we were talking about: how to add more materials and elements that will allow us to continue toward that horizon. And I think that this dynamic of change forces us all to go through that process.

This all became very clear to me because I had been traveling, and when I returned, I noticed a certain discrepancy among the comrades who wanted to understand what happened and could not figure out how to do so. We have to give ourselves time to find our own way of moving forward.

Many people tell us: "now you have to do this, you have to do that," but I think we have to find our own way. That means first as the MTD of Solano and later sharing it with the Aníbal Verón. It is a major challenge. Many comrades are demanding this, and they demand it in individual, smaller spaces, but I think that we have to find a way to do it among everyone. If not, some comrades will get left behind.

Does that illusion that you mentioned consist of thinking that everything has been resolved, that it is no longer necessary to keep searching?

I think that sometimes different realities get mixed up. For example, our principles are very similar to those of the Zapatistas, but we are very different organizations. They have had time to develop and mature, which allowed them to consolidate things. The situation in the urban periphery is very different. Sometimes I think about how the question of how radical you can be is in contradiction with our very real situation of how exposed we are. Definitively, they are armed, they are an army, they have their anonymity in their favor. In our case, our organization is open, permeable to any type of investigation, because they must know us like the back of their hands. They go to an assembly and listen. So, sometimes there is an illusion that turns into an idealization of the principles. This is a very clear difference between a proposal for counter-power and other types of politics: there are many organizations that propose pushing the situation to its limits, sharpening the contradictions, to then go on the counter-offensive. But that involves a huge idealization of what we are.

That is the strategy of some organizations that openly propose increasing the level of violence so that people realize that something has to be done. Two dead, five, ten, or twenty injured, two hundred people arrested: "that is fuel for struggle" they say to us. These organizations don't have any social support, nor do they even have the operating capacity to carry out what they declare, they try to outdo you from the left, they accuse you of being rigid, of holding back the struggle by protecting your project.

The experience of Latin America, in this sense, is graphic. In Guatemala there were a hundred and fifty thousand deaths, in Nicaragua I don't know how many, a few thousand in El Salvador. Entire communities have been massacred. I think the issue of bursting bubbles, getting rid of illusions, thinking about who we are, what we want, is important, because we don't all think in the same way. It is true that the situation often forces you to go out and protest all the time, and we get into a cycle of activity that destroys the possibilities for us to affirm ourselves in what we want.

We cannot call for silence, we have to scream loudly for them to hear us. Perhaps that is another advantage the Zapatistas have.

But that is not exactly an objective advantage: you have to have a lot of courage and firmness to be able to call for silence after a caravan like that and having been in the absolute center of Mexican politics. The question seems to be how to thwart that game of power, of what is expected of you, how to throw it into disarray and confusion.

Yes, especially because you have to put up with criticism from those people who don't want to do things themselves, that spend all their time waiting for someone who will do those things, and then place conditions on them.

9. The acceleration of temporalities and the electoral conjuncture: "they all must go"[29]

When Zamora called for the gathering and journalists commented that the Aníbal Verón Coordinator would be present, we started receiving all types of messages: some congratulating us and others trying to convince us that we shouldn't go.

If not for the very specific circumstances, we would not have issued the communique that we published then. We would have preferred silence. But there were two circumstances that forced us to make a declaration. On the one hand, because the comrades from another MTD in the Verón had approached the meeting; and, even though they had clarified that they were only going to listen, that they were not participating as an organization, the media started saying that the Verón was one of the organizations calling the meeting. On the other hand, there were comrades in the Verón who did not come to debate the position that we were going to take among everyone because they had already decided to go to one of the activities that was being organized, which took place on the Pueyrredón Bridge. In that context, if we did not say anything, others were going to start speaking for us.

It was tough because there was a lot of debate, especially around the issue of how that statement could generate more isolation just as we were facing a lot of repression.

---

29   A few days before this encounter, there was a call for a mobilization to Congress in the framework of a broader action plan called by Luis Zamora, Elisa Carrió, and Victor De Gennaro to demand immediate elections for all elected positions and the resignation of all deputies and senators. The campaign was launched with the slogan – which emerged during the days of protest on December 19th and 20th: "all of them must go," and was supported by many popular organizations (including many neighborhood assemblies). Nonetheless, at that time, the Aníbal Verón Coordinator did not participate in the gathering and sent out a communiqué explaining the motives for their absence. The appearance of this communiqué unleashed an intense debate between those that criticized with the Verón's decision and those that shared their judgment.

But we know that the electoral dynamic places us in a different scenario. Many of the sectors with whom we have been fighting alongside are placing all their energy in the electoral arena. This weakens us in the popular field.

There is something else too. We think that the repressive situation is intensifying. And the problem is that this repression occurs through different means.

One of the means is what they tried on June 26: killing our comrades. They wanted to start something with us that later they would surely continue with other organizations and struggles. That time, luckily, it failed, and the repression was put on hold for a while. Now it is intensifying considerably in the neighborhoods but in a more subtle way.

Another element that we see as an act of repression is institutional repression and this worries us just as much as the former. This has to do with how they institutionalize and legitimate struggles *for* the state and not *from* organizations. We would have been out on the streets if the call had been to denounce what is happening in the neighborhoods, the pressure being placed on organizations, the attempts to evict Brukman and Zanon, etc. That is the terrain on which we have to elaborate popular proposals and slogans that have depth and meaning, such as the anti-repressive struggle, or the "they all must go," that arose from different places and which no organization can claim as their own or claim to have the privileged interpretation.

We are not interested in these slogans, which have a lot of meaning today, being used for electoral purposes. Even more so, we think that it is the most acute form of repression that they are using and that it would be dangerous for us to fall into that trap. We already know how Carrió and De Gennaro work, and while we like and respect Zamora, we think that he is making a mistake. We would like to be able to talk about it with him, to explain how we see things.

That is what we refer to as a very subtle form of repression: putting us in that quandary that does not respect our own times and spaces.

We should clarify that we didn't want to say anything because we didn't have anything to say in that situation, since many people think that when we stay quiet or don't take the streets, it is because we have too much pride. But, at the same time, if we do say something, they call us sectarian. Their interpretation is they helped us when we were in a painful situation and now, we are turning our backs on them. If we had to go out and protest when they killed our comrades Dario and Maxi, it is because repression affects all of us: they come for us today and tomorrow for others.

The fundamental point of what we were trying to say in the communique is that we do not organize according to the electoral calendar, but according to our temporality.

We heard a militant from a leftist party say that the groups that make up the Aníbal Verón are authoritarian because they don't allow political parties to participate. But we have a different reason: we know that political parties are always going to look for a way to assimilate you into their logic. The same thing happens when they tell us that we need them when there is repression and that later we don't respond to their calls. But we see it differently. When we blocked all the bridges in response to the repression in Mosconi, we don't send them a bill or tell them they owe us something. We would never do that. It is because when it comes to matters of repression there is no distinction. They want to put everything in the same box and say that this call, for a mobilization that has to do with their political vision, is the same as an event such as the massacre on June 26.

That moment activated a sense that now everything has to do with the electoral issue. We are not seeking isolation, but in those types of practices we are necessarily going to suffer a certain isolation as long as this electoral conjuncture lasts. Because it is not essential to us, and we are not going to go around thinking about it all the time. When many people are proposing that, in the face of repression, we have to accelerate things to continue advancing against power, we think precisely the opposite: that we have to consolidate experiences, deepen our relationships with comrades. It is a very different time and place. Therefore, people are going to look at us even more, because this is going to mark even more profound differences.

Not only did they criticize us for not participating, but we also received many calls from groups that are part of the very organizations that called the gathering saying that they agreed with our position and many assemblies invited us to come explain how we see things. It is something that never ends because anything that we do will become public. The other problem is that there are also differences within the Verón, and that forces us to have to speak out because we feel trapped and find ourselves immersed in this dynamic of coming and going. But what matters is that we don't allow this to take away our dreams, and knowing that, until the elections are over, we are going to get shaken up by a ton of circumstances that we should not allow to leave us in despair.

10.   The diffused network

We have tried to analyze the connections between experiences of counter-power through the idea of a diffused network. We mentioned this to you all at some point, however, we still are not clear how you understand this issue...

It is a matter of understanding that we don't need this type of unity that is so often declared in the name of resisting domination. We always hear: "we are just missing the tools," in other words, the unity of command from which all types of indications emerge "so that the people in their orphanage…" That command is thought of as a type of leadership, although many pose it as something collective, it always ends up as leadership of a few. We understand that each experience has to develop its potentiality, its creativity, and that articulation is only possible through those types of networks in which nobody directs anyone, but rather we all come together in a confluence in certain settings. That is what we do with MOCASE: the comrades come and tell us about their victories, their challenges, and, of course, we create a relationship of solidarity and articulation because we can see that they are also working from below, in very concrete ways. But it would never occur to us to tell the MOCASE what they should do, or to tell comrades from Mosconi what would be best for them. For us, the connections and relationships that are generated in these exchanges that are enough for us: we don't need a central command or any other type of tool. We agree that there is no need for a centralization of power or a place in which politics is elaborated to then take it to places that are not capable of elaborating it: that would go against our principles of organization. Looking at it based on what we don't want and what we are doing, I think that we can affirm ourselves in that type of relation: through autonomy and for autonomy. We don't posit it in terms of a diffused network. We understand those relationships, those connections, in terms of coordination and articulation.

At a certain point in time, the image of the network started being used all over the place: there was a call to "build through networks." Everyone started thinking of everything as "networked." We all took up that image very quickly. So, we started asking ourselves why the concept of the "network" is so attractive. We started to perceive – with the help of some friends who were also looking at all of this – that the "alternative networks" facilitated antagonistic forms of popular organization because they were in opposition to another "network": the financial network, the mass media network, the informational, cybernetic, and institutional network that operates at the foundation of contemporary domination, as well as the mafia networks, the para-police networks, drug trafficking networks, networks of corruption. Suddenly, everything was operating as a network. Then, when we confirmed this "similarity," we started asking up to what point these networks should be considered equivalent. Because, while, on one hand, the image of the network can guide us in building in decentralized and non-hierarchical ways, on the other hand, accepting these networked forms seemed suspicious to us, precisely because it reproduces the current forms of domination.

This suspicion is very complex because, in reality, capital – which increasingly operates in networked forms – has adopted these forms by copying them from other experiences such as the organization of mafia, drug trafficking, or revolutionary cells. But, once domination takes up this networked form, it is still necessary to reflect on the implications for alternative networks.

The slogan "organize the world in a network," is now the slogan of domination. But we are not interested in opposing that network of domination to an alternative "network," that would also connect as many points as possible.

Perhaps the slogan should not be "all points tend to connect," but rather to think in terms of resonance: in other words, that each site in which new meanings are being constructed can finally expand, resonate, compose with others, beyond any demands that are external to this constituent becoming. These knots of intensity have an enormous potential to produce something else, another way of relating to one another, other ideas, another subjectivity, and that cannot be guaranteed by the simple act of adhering to an explicit network.

In this sense, experience tells us that each time a network is explicitly organized that seeks to organize the entire diffused network in which points of potencia are unfolding, groups and people appear that say "I am part of this" and they tend to become detached from the experience of intensity in which they had been involved to start to work "for the network."

So, we see the (diffused) network as the opposite of a completely organized network. The diffused network speaks to us of many types of encounters, many partially explicit, limited, overlapping networks, of different modes of articulation, coordination, ultimately as many networks as becomings to be able to open up the experience in question. In that sense, it seems fundamental to not be trapped in only one main network that tends to organize and create hierarchies among the multiplicity that any experience opens up to us.

There are different types of articulation and different types of coordination, emerging from different areas of organizing, without the struggle having one unified direction, as is traditional. We are in the Aníbal Verón Coordinator and the COPA. Now we are also trying to generate encounters for autonomous thought with different organizations that have proposed building social change through autonomy in very different contexts. What is important is that we don't integrate all these spaces into one single network, but we simply coordinate and articulate based on agreements and objectives.

It seems that the most important aspects of the affinities between experiences do not have to do with the commonly used arguments about "unity." Rather, it is a matter, for example, of knowing that the MOCASE and the MTD of Solano are doing the same thing in very different situations. When this happens, you don't need ten hours of meetings to confirm that you think exactly the same about each point. Often the practice itself demonstrates similarities that would be ruined if you were to sit down and explain or write about them. We are already very well aware that we can all be mistrusting of discourse: it can be accommodating, but the values deployed in practices clearly either attract or repel us. We perceive this affinity as a feeling of falling in love or friendship, and we think that it is much more powerful than any other type of utilitarian relation, for the sake of convenience, subject to a strategy.

The encounter that we had this week – and that ended with the march to the Plaza de Mayo – with comrades from MOCASE, APENOC, farmers from Mendoza, and other groups, was that type of experience. Because we clearly have known each other for a long time, through the *Situaciones* booklets, or through dialogues in other space, such as COPA, and it always seemed that we had very similar forms of constructing: although we work in very different contexts, we do something similar in terms of organizing principles and criteria. We would always say, "we need to sit down and talk," but we were never able to make it happen. It was now, without thinking too much about it, without planning it, based on a concrete need, that the opportunity emerged for this space of encounter. The organizations that participated spent two entire days together and we have been greatly strengthened by it.

What you were saying speaks to this experience of what we have called "intensity" or "resonance," which is nothing other than the experiences that organize friendships between projects or that "creates relationships" between different experiments. Because it could be that you have this feeling of friendship with, to take as an example, the MOCASE, but the MOCASE has that feeling with another project that doesn't speak to you. Any attempt to "close off" the possible connections in the name of affirming a political identity ends with impoverishment and disaster. The discussions start drifting into criteria for belonging – who should enter and who should leave – the levels of belonging and their limits; ultimately, it restricts the possibilities.

On the contrary, the network "of resonances" can be very broad even if – and perhaps because – these connections cannot be explained: why is there so much affinity with a certain group and not another? These affinities cannot always be rationalized in a common strategy. They cannot always be reduced to a calculation.

The explicit networks, those that are effectively structured, can be very useful for a particular objective, for a precise moment – in the long or short term – and they don't encompass the (diffused) network. But when one of those structured networks claims to be "the" strategic network, that seeks to organize all the others, a process of centralization and hierarchy begins that, on the one hand, is an attack against horizontality and internal democracy and, on the other hand – and this is the determining aspect for us – closes off networks and situations that will not subordinate themselves to it.

We propose strategic objectives that go beyond feelings and friendship, but without the pretense of being the enlightened vanguard. When we speak of social change, we are thinking in strategic terms, outlining a horizon.

In some way, the explicit network is the crutch that we have access to in cases of aggression: it is about feeling that we are part of something bigger to be able to defend the organization. I think that this moment of constant aggression from the system conditions our construction to a large degree. The need to make these spaces explicit has to do with avoiding those types of attacks; it is part of our self-defense. It does not determine us, but it does condition us. It is almost a survival instinct of the projects that are building in the midst of a ton of limitations. Furthermore, the aggressiveness with which the system tries to annihilate us forces us to take up that type of crutch, thus it is a limit that we face.

What do you all mean by the diffused network?

Perhaps we could say that the diffused network expands based on the multiplicity of affinities and that these are constantly being renewed, increasing, as well as diminishing, in number and intensity. In this sense, the pretense to organize all these flows of sympathy is necessarily condemned to failure, because these bonds can never be trapped in utilitarian molds: sympathy, affinity, love are dynamic, mutating, and combative terms that resist being stacked up and manipulated. Therefore, we propose the idea of a diffused network that it is not opposed to or in contradiction with the explicit network, but is its more radical foundation.

When we establish coordinating bodies and articulation, we do so based on agreements that are grounded in common interests and objectives. We would have to think seriously about where the intention to generate networks comes from. We can think about the experience of the MTD of Solano itself, in how the different neighborhoods that are organized in the movement are articulated together. It is very clear how, sometimes, due to issues of education, plans, one ends up co-opting the experience of another neighborhood, homogenizing and unifying all the wealth that can be found in the emergence of an MTD. There are times when we cut off experiences that are very rich that respond to particularities of neighborhoods that are very different. In each community, each neighborhood, each of the MTD's spaces, there are multiple experiences, and some are similar and others are not. The question is: how can we build starting from these experiences toward common objectives, for everyone?

We have been maturing a lot in this sense recently, because we have realized that many of the criteria and guidelines that we had put forth had to do with that element of wanting to use an organization to control different experiences that are out of our hands. Here the issue of autonomy appears again: On what basis do we think that a determined practice has to developed and strengthened? It is truly a very rich discussion.

11. Maximum creation, minimum control

The weakness of traditional political militants lies in the desire to be a specialist in controlling what they build, in administrating it.

But furthermore, in a type of dogmatic thought, the recipe cannot be altered: "if the same thing is not repeated, then something is wrong." For us, it is a much richer experience if the same thing is not repeated: with autonomy, real democracy, participation, counter-power.

It is crucially necessary to take responsibility for the fact that there is no external criteria of coherence, no impartial judge that would be able to evaluate an experience's validity, saying "what is going on in neighborhoods A and B needs to be coherent, taking what I say, of course, as a point of coherence." If you take that path, it ends up into constantly forcing reality into a particular box, the name of "popular power," "counter-power," or what have you. Obviously, it ends it up blocking the potency and potential of those experiences, without being able to recognize up to what point an authentic experience does not fit into any type of model.

Putting forth a collective project raises questions of the exercise of freedom, and we differentiate between freedom, liberty, and liberalism. Freedom implies collective constructions – based on common interests – and change. Liberalism means going at it alone. While each organization in each neighborhood has its own specificities and different processes, there are collective problems, such as unemployment, poverty, misery, repression, caused by the same system that attacks all of us. In order to fight against all of that, and to build something new, it is necessary to organize based on collective agreements. The struggle is collective. One thing is for certain and that is that, within this collective struggle, there are very different experiences, and that is why recipes will not work.

We have many examples: we saw it with the workshop coordination. A model for the productive workshops was created that pushed the same methodology in each neighborhood, when the subjectivities of the comrades are different in each place. For example, they put the same criteria on a project that started four years ago as one with comrades who just started working four months ago.

This is something that we discussed with the members of Popular Escrache Organizing Committee: they maintain a critical distance with the escraches carried out by the assemblies,[30] they don't see the "generalization" of the escrache as the success of a type of struggle that they, to a certain extent, introduced.[31] For the Committee, the assemblies' escraches are "something else" (without judging them) since they belong to situations and senses that are not immediately the same. Thus, the generalization of a form of struggle does not automatically imply the same network nor the possibility of a common experience.

Because the escrache – introduced by H.I.J.O.S – was developed in the struggle against the theory of the two demons[32] as a very situational and subtle hypothesis in a specific context: it functioned as a machine for the production of popular justice.

The assemblies used the escrache in another context. This is not, we insist, a value judgment, but rather an exercise of distinguishing contexts, the difference meanings of two moments of escrache.

Something similar can happen based on the confirmation that even though all the piqueterx organizations obviously carry out piquetes, they are not all the same, nor do their roadblocks all mean the same thing.

---

30   *Escrache* refers to a type of direct action usually held in front someone's home or workplace. The tactic was originally used by human rights organizations, such as HIJOS (the sons and daughters of those disappeared by the military dictatorship), to shed light on those responsible for the crimes against humanity during the dictatorship. Thus, they became a form of popular justice, often involving street theater and people's tribunals, at a time when there was still official impunity for those crimes. The tactic was later taken up and replicated by other movements, for example neighborhood assemblies that used them to call out government officials and corporate leaders responsible for the violence of neoliberalism. – Trans.

31   This was one of the problems that was analyzed in the pamphlet *Situaciones 5: Assassin in the Neighborhood. The committee of Popular Escrache* (Buenos Aires: De mano en mano, 2002).

32   The "theory of two demons" refers to the idea that in Argentina there was a "dirty war" with violence ("demons") on "both sides": the military dictatorship and the guerrilla forces and other resistance movements. This theory has largely been discredited in the popular imagination due to the work of human rights organizations to show that there was no equivalency between state violence and violence exercised by the resistance. – Trans.

In this sense, the diffused network is also an image that enables putting that multiplication of senses and meanings into play, impeding the imposition of a single criteria for measuring the value of what is being done.

For us, it is important to think about what experiences lie behind each action. It is true that there are many, and very different, *escraches* and *piquetes*, but the novelty can be found in what is being constructed subjectively in order to be able to carry out each action. Carrying out an *escrache* against Edenor demanding that they improve their service is not the same as one denouncing them for being thieves and complicit with the repressive state. The same goes for a factory takeover: proposing workers' management is not the same thing as demanding nationalization. Making a call to recuperate what was stolen from us is not the same thing as requesting nationalization of, for example, YPF [Yacimientos Petrolíferos Fiscales] and the oil, because that would just be changing one master for another. The state is part of the system of domination.

In this sense, we have to constantly revise what we are doing, because it is an experiment and we are always being conditioned. That is, even though we have certain principles of construction, there is a constant tension between expressing them one way and practicing them another. It is not only a matter of expressing them verbally, but also building them in practice: that is the struggle.

While there is a lot of freedom in this experience, it is no less true that we are in a situation in which it is necessary to constantly revise our agreements in order to not reproduce that capitalism that has so deeply infused everyday life and that distorts the horizons that we propose traveling toward.

The freedom of "everything is possible," corresponding to capitalism, cannot be the same as the freedom that is produced in the experience of the subjective creation of social bonds. Both call themselves "freedom," but they are fundamentally opposed to one another.

In fact, the freedom that they talk about is that which says that each one of us is a complete individual and that nothing would be better for each of us than to "voluntarily" choose dispersion.

But multiplicity is not dispersion. And the freedom of creating, that which provides us with an ethics of struggle, is not freedom of individualism.

This is very delicate subject, because, in general, the response to individualism and dispersion is to centralize with authority, with hierarchy. That is clearly what the market achieves: everyone is "free," everyone is "dispersed," that is to say, everyone "ordered in a hierarchy," and "separated."

But for many people who do "serious politics," identifying "multiplicity" and "dispersion" as problems is inevitable. Therefore, they end up calling for more "organization," reducing, as much as possible, the role of autonomous production of practices and chosen forms of relation.

This critique came out after our publication of Situaciones 4: they reproached us, saying it is not possible to make a "happy island" in the midst of the shit, and that an experience like this one would only up not caring about everyone else.

But our way of understanding freedom implies the exact opposite, because if there is one thing that kills creativity, that destroys the possibility of building knowledge and thought, it is precisely generating those diagrams. The possibility of have to create everything again must be tremendously anxiety-producing after having spent years and centuries managing everything with programs, with diagrams. They say: "if we had everything so well planned, why doesn't it work?" That is precisely what kills everything; that is the problem, because it is impossible to have everything defined when human experiences are changing every day. How could you predict that? You cannot, and if you try to, you end up imposing a conservative sense, there is no other option. That's how we reproduce those relations of domination. And that is what historically does not work: when there is already a program and you end up obeying. That is the logic of capitalism: dominated-dominator. Many traditional political parties have trouble understanding this. However, for us, it gives a sensation of freedom, because it shows that yes, it is possible to build things differently, that there are new possibilities every day and that you will encounter new hypotheses, new proposals.

12. The production of world(s)

This brings us to ask you how you see the slogan from the anti-globalization movement, "another world is possible." Sometimes we get the impression that this – well-intentioned – phrase over-simplifies. Because the image of "changing the world" implies that there is already an indisputable ideal to which "the world" should fit to, and whose idea is that? Therefore, we think that it could be better said as the production of world(s), of creating expansive, intensive experiences, that involve a very concrete "being in the world."

The idea of "changing the world" could hide – even without meaning to – another simplification: the existence of a "we who are good," those of us who have the best intentions. But who would feel outside of this group? What would be the mechanisms for making the world conform to those good intentions? If one thing is certain it is that "the world" (if that unity exists as such) is not so simple to manipulate, but rather is too complex to be molded at one's pleasure. What can be done, on the other hand, is to produce experiences, and we can produce ourselves as something else.

Of course, proposing this implies subjecting yourself to the moral blackmail that repeats: "but, how?" "we want a 'good world' and you all come to tell us that it doesn't make sense to talk about 'that?': wouldn't that make you all the reactionaries who are opposed to that good world?"

But the other issue is that this slogan can even "save" what could be changed from this world, since it doesn't submit to criticism this idea of what is "good" – for the coming world – and therefore what would be the "bad" that would have to be repudiated. But what happens with the values that emerge based on practices that refuse to accommodate themselves to the ideal being promoted and instead deal with the complexity and lack of a coherent unity of the "world" on an everyday basis?

There is another problem: that "another world is possible" can also be understood as saying that another type of capitalism is possible. The slogan is so broad that it could you allow you to think that capitalism could be reformed: changing some characters, generating some values. But we remain prisoners to the same logic of construction.

I prefer the slogan "a world where many worlds are possible." Because if philosophers start imagining the world for us, I think there will be problems. But I like "a world in which many worlds are possible" because it expresses the multiplicity of experiences, as well as tolerance. Singular thinking, believing there is only one way of thinking, has already caused a lot of damage, on both sides. It has not recognized cultural diversity. Unfortunately, this also happened to the Church, which understood unity as uniformity of thought and cultural repression: that is empire, imperialism. The Church continued to use Latin because it thought it was that was the way to generate unity and in Latin America, they encountered a wealth of Indigenous languages and it was more difficult for them.

Understanding unity as uniformity has caused a lot of harm. Thinking of "a" world would be messed up. But understanding the unity of coexistence, even with the different and the varied, will require a process of maturation: to accept the distinct, the different, as long as it does not harm the collective. We could also say that in this search for a new sociability, anything that does not harm the collective is good. Because it could also be "give me the right to be different, and then I keep oppressing you, give me the right to exploit you." That's the limit, those are capitalism's mottoes.

Furthermore, I don't know if another world is possible, because the possibles that can be conceived and active are the worlds that exist. I think there is a general and very ideological view that says, "I don't like capitalism; therefore, another world is possible." But if another world is possible, it is because it exists as seeds; if not, it is not possible and is nothing more than an idea. What I mean is that if the alternative world to capitalism is a world we are dreaming of, it clearly has less force, less realness, less multiplicity than the existing one. On the other hand, what already exists as something else has a material force that can be constituted into desirable realities for other people. These realities are much more powerful than any ideal. And not in the sense that there is an ideal that is internal to the experience that is what moves it. What is interesting about these experiences is not the idea of what they should be, but rather that they already exist, as real, social experiments.

The vast majority of the comrades in the movement started because they had had enough. Only a few comrades joined the movement because they feel it, due to desire. The majority only approached us because they were trying to get by, to survive, and if they find work they will go straight back to the factory, because that is the ideal world sold to us by capitalism: the world of exploited labor.

Christianity would say: "we suffer now and one day we will arrive to paradise, that place where we will finally be happy and reach our full potential." Some authors say that human beings need horizons, utopias, and I think that is true, as long as that utopia is not an impediment. Because what happens is that, by seeing everything on such a universal level, it inhibits the real possibilities for acting on them now. This can create obstacles for embodying the challenge of creating, because if you think about it three times, you probably won't do it. Reason can kill practice. I think that this happens with ideology, which, in a certain moment, proclaimed that we were about to arrive, and when that entered into crisis, many people went out and said, "no, it is not possible." It is as if we were to sit down to think about what we're going to be doing in five years: it is very likely that thinking that way would inhibit us.

Furthermore, we have had the experience: we saw how those constituted meanings came undone. Before you used to know that if you were a worker, you would be able to go to the union to fight, to gain more power for the class (or the party) and to organize the world according to that new power.

Nonetheless, some people have not acknowledged those changes and think that the revolution will occur through general strikes.

Another vision which can – involuntarily – be reactionary is the discourse that reduces everything that is being created to an effect of "necessity," such as when they say that the piqueterx movement exists because there are people who need work. This cannot be denied: it is very true that there is a lack of jobs. But, with such an economistic vision, many of the possible alternatives are reduced to a single one, organized based on the dominant responses. The example is clear: if we conclude that "an unemployed person wants a job" we lose sight of an immense number of possibilities, that are opened up in the realm of the situation, but closed off by the ideology of necessity, that is external to the situation and tries to establish "rational solutions." But, of course, everything we have been talking about offers an infinite number of other examples: if school becomes a problem for the kids in the MTD, possibilities open up connected to the capacity and desire for creation; in that case, it opens the possibility for a school that is more connected to the demands of existence determined by the struggle that is being waged.

In this sense, it is clear that the MTD brings together people who want to live differently: to struggle against individualism, alcoholism... There is a desire to live. That is a very important point that always escapes the "ideology of necessity" that floods the political discourse, like when they say that everything that is happening now is only because we are going through an exceptional moment of "economic crisis."

These experiences don't only exist because of the economic crisis, but also because of the breakdown of sociability and belonging to spheres that are much bigger than one's own family group. The fear and isolation that provoked this collapse are sickening: when you cannot relate to your loved ones and your acquaintances, a fracture begins to form that is also experienced as a loss. Therefore, I think that the recuperation of spaces with something more socializing, where it is possible to establish relations, is being experienced by many people and many families as a very intensive recuperation, that goes beyond purely economic issues. In Latin America, the sense of community is very strong and is being recovered despite the pressure that is placed on those cores. That is the art of capitalism, dividing people into parts.

Going back to what we were in talking about in terms of diffused networks, it seems to me that we are creating something like parallel societies. Because, with this need to materially (re)produce life, increasingly turning to invention, self-valorization, and autonomy, the challenge arises of how to produce things that do not end up reproducing a mirror of capitalism. Obviously, it is not a matter of establishing "refuges" or "uncontaminated" places. But, precisely for that reason, we will have to be sufficiently creative to maintain the experience of existence as something "open," resisting anything that would try to "close" it. In that sense, the idea of another world runs that paradoxical risk: it could end up closing more than it opens.

Organizing criteria and principles make sense and are meaningful when they are sustained in practice: if they are emptied of content, they can deeply harm the organization. We often want to see comrades obligatorily respond to those principles, without giving them the chance or the necessary tools to choose, to decide, "to be part of" the MTD. To be able to act, you have to have a desire, if not, the comrade, or often even the collective itself, will be harmed. You have to make the experience your own.

Epilogue

1. Horizontality is a practical wager

Some of us had been militants before our experience in the MTD; in other words, we brought things from prior experiences with us. The first thing that we had to do was to learn how to listen to each other: the struggle that we wanted to advance, the problems we were facing, and the dignity we wanted to recuperate. Thus, we spent time learning and searching for creative ways to move forward in that path.

From the beginning, we saw that it was necessary to build something new, based on our own situation, something that we all had to be part of. That is why notions of autonomy, horizontality, democracy, and the comprehensive struggle have emerged. We didn't invent them: the only thing we did was listen and take on the reality that we were facing.

Recently, talking about something similar, we said that memory, identity, and hope engender many practices and it is matter of figuring out how to recover and develop them. Horizontality is embedded in the movement's everyday practice and we started shaping and organizing it collectively. It was something that we took up very naturally. For example, we do not have leaders because together we learned that leaders are not useful for us, that if we don't do things together, it won't work.

Horizontality involves a different way of relating to others, a new way of discovering possibilities for changing reality. When you are in a situation, you can have hypotheses, solutions, responses, but they are always personal. They are positions that usually change when we work collectively. It has to do with a willingness to constantly learn, to accept that what you thought was true will change when you work collectively. This is not only related to self-organization and self-management, but rather – and primarily – with defining ourselves: that is, not allowing anyone or anything else to dictate who we are, but rather discovering for ourselves who we are and how we are going to transform reality.

Horizontality is a practice tied to a project. It is not a concept that can be understood on its own, but rather a way of relating to others that depends on a concrete practice. Therefore, it has to do with relationships in different directions and not directed toward above or below. Proposing to build from below to reach the top implies a contradiction with horizontality. That is why we try to no longer use the concept "from below."

2. Autonomy: power of doing and thinking of freedom

Autonomy is the project that we chose to build. We understand our problems, their causes, and we are able to create solutions by reflecting and learning together as comrades.

We know who we are: people who are able to transform reality through creative and liberating work, without the need for exploitation. The space that we build is based on new relations, which are radically opposed to the capitalist system that we know is what we don't want. By confronting everyday reality and acting on it, a new subjectivity is born, a new way of thinking: free and collective. Based on how we define ourselves, we collectively organize and manage ourselves.

The MTD Solano's experiment is not the only one that poses the question of autonomy. The space of construction of autonomous thought is made up of many organizations: MTDs, neighborhood assemblies, students, and cultural groups. At the same time, we form connections with other spaces, such as Indigenous and peasant groups.

We are motivated by this new thing that we are experiencing. That new way of working is prioritized within the movement, in which there is a new puzzle to solve every day and, since it is new, we have to think about it a lot. It is difficult because it is a constant unknown: How do we make productive projects? There is no program. Nor are we interested in confronting this lack of definition, because what we are doing is constituting a horizon that is not a goal, but rather a path that we are walking, as we build it, and, at the same time, encountering the questions that arise. Our satisfaction has to do with having a blank piece of paper and putting a small dot on it.

This comes up all the time. For example, when we held the bonfires to generate collective spirit, in which we gathered around the fire to say a thought and throw in little sticks that fuel the fire, the "militants" had difficulties coming up with something of their own to say; meanwhile, our comrades would say something of their own right away and throw in their stick. What was going on? They didn't have to ask themselves what phrase would have the greatest impact, or who to quote. For the "militant" comrades, on the other hand, the blank page was already written, and they got lost trying to find a quote from Che or Marx.

We are discovering the meaning of freedom collectively, and it is very different from the liberalism of capitalism. As a people, we liberate ourselves from domination, subjugation, exploitation, and we ground ourselves in the common good, rejecting individualism, selfishness, and prioritizing personal rather than collective interests.

In the midst of overwhelming poverty and an entire institutional structure that always tries to destroy spaces of freedom, we have been able to generate that space of freedom: freedom to think, to practice and make mistakes, to correct our errors and start over, and to share our dreams – dreams that are always frustrated, because we live in a repressive society. That is very difficult to measure.

3. A project of projects

In this sense, our project of building a school is closely tied to that space of freedom. A school cannot become a bubble that protects children from an adverse reality. Many organizations try to do that: they try to construct another world there, in the school. We think of the school as just another one of MTD's spaces, a space that will not be easy because the intention is to empower creation and freedom. But we do not want to educate children who later grow up and find themselves lost in a hostile world, rather our aspiration is that the children experience their freedom there with a critical consciousness. Our project involves generating a space that strengthens the commitment to live critically in a world such as our current one.

Primary school was traditionally thought of as a step before high school, and high school as the prelude to the university: the formula to get a job. The new generations today, especially those kids from the urban periphery, even if they graduate, do not find anything. Thinking that these kids will have more opportunities because they study is a lie. Nonetheless, it is not a matter of telling those kids not to study, but that they can start practicing collective work from a young age, that they can find a trade or profession in which they can integrate their own knowledges with collective knowledge.

When we think of school, the question of horizontality arises again. We cannot allow ourselves to fall into the trap of being a group of adults who end up imposing a kind of education on children without taking into account what they are going through, their own experiences. In other words, a school must be thought up *with* the children, not *for* the children. We can often see in them what we are constructing: when they play at being in a roadblock, a march, or an assembly, or they come together in a game workshop or in the *murga*, and define how they want to play and what they want to do. That is what they are showing us: how to think about school and not just respond to the faults that we have identified in state schools.

For us, there can be no horizontality without autonomy, and there is a complex relationship between them. Decisions are often made in horizontal spaces that run counter to the organization's principles. Sometimes the horizontal mechanism produces something negative. That is why we say that horizontality on its own does not make sense, it must be tied to true autonomy, that is, the freedom to build something. For us, all of these things are connected and integral to the struggle.

After June 26, when many people turned around to observe us and we started making public the ways in which we work – that is, when the generalized support commenced – our feeling was the same as that described by Ringo Bonavena: "the whole world applauds you when you go into the ring, but once you are up there you are left all alone." They even take away your bench.

What we care about is that those who are applauding us also engage in the experience of moving out of their comfort zone, going beyond what they are used to, that vertical structure in which we are generally all embedded and that they carry out a different type of work. In other words, that they stop being spectators.

4. Prolonging words

After publishing the pamphlet *Situaciones 4,* we received a lot of criticism regarding what we said about taking power. That was to be expected.

It also provoked debates within the MTD, in the sense that what we said there is not always accomplished in everyday practice. That is, faced with our internal tensions, the material functions as the starting point for a debate, a reference for the things that we think but that we do not always carry out in practice.

Perhaps we needed to clarify that our experience is not perfect. Perhaps we should have clarified that the criteria that we explained in that publication have not yet been achieved and are still being worked on, it is no simple and easy matter. We have a lot of problems with the productive projects, for example, and, once again, horizontality is difficult to deploy practically.

It is clear that anyone who idealizes is mistaken: all experiences are difficult and it is impossible to say that we *already* have a "horizontal and democratic" organization and all those things that, of course, we aim for every day. In that sense, the pamphlet was useful in that it allowed us to disclose an experience that otherwise would have remained unknown because the media is not interested in giving space to those thoughts.

We have also heard the criticism, coming from within the Aníbal Verón, that the MTD of Solano are the only ones who appear, when we are not the only ones in the struggle. We respond by saying that this occurred in a moment when many of us were thinking about these things and it was a way of working through them. Furthermore, for our organization, it was a moment in which we thought it was necessary to speak out, in our own voice, and that voice is not so easy: there is the media and what they show of us, which is not what we are. Lastly, other organizations have even labeled us "situationists." We respond to this claim by saying that we have our own voice and our own experience. But is clear that many of these ideas that we support seem like a kick in the gut to them. Furthermore, those criticisms have to do with the well-known custom of interpreting everything according to a theoretical framework, an attitude with which it is impossible to understand an experience that is not subject to any of the pre-established frameworks. It is that imperious need to label and classify everything in order to be able to manipulate it. Many people had difficulty classifying us; at first, they had labeled us "anarchists." When this pamphlet came out, then they found the perfect moniker, "ah, they are situationists or Negrians!" In any case, it doesn't bother us at all. But it makes us laugh when they say, "hey, that guy is sort of situationist, is he not?" or "your friends the situationists."

MTD-Solano, September 2002